This is a book for Christians serious enough to truly believe that God is God and that He accomplishes His ends through means consistent with His nature. It will not be popular with those who feel secretly that God has let the world down and that they must do what He has neglected to do. I thank Dean Merrill for saying boldly what deeply troubles many Christians about the politicized message of many of our very sincere brothers and sisters in Christ. This is a book worth reading in these troubled times. It will help us to avoid hand-wringing as well as flailing anger.

Dr. Jay Kesler, President
Taylor University

In today's cultural fragmentation, how can Christians make a difference? Not, says Merrill, by adopting the world's methods but by returning to and following New Testament models. A timely, provocative contribution to today's discussions.

Harold Myra, President
Christianity Today, Inc.

I highly recommend this carefully documented and intriguingly illustrated book, which offers the "light" of a truly biblical alternative to the "heat" generated by much of the inflamed rhetoric used by Christians in our present-day culture wars.

In *Sinners in the Hands of an Angry Church*, Dean Merrill has his hand on the pulse of the condition within our evangelical community. This book is a must for many of us who need to be reminded that the state of our nation is not a surprise to God or a task for God. In this war, He is the general and we get our marching orders from Him.

Dr. John M. Perkins
Founder, Harambee Christian Family Center,
Harambee Preparatory School
Chairman, Christian Community Development Association

I only hope it will transform your outlook as much as it has mine.

David A. Seamands
Author and Counselor

This book is a "must" for anyone who wants to put faith to work in the political arena. It is readable, balanced, informative and insightful. It spells out a biblical style for engaging the principalities and powers of our day.

Tony Campolo
Professor of Sociology
Eastern College

Dean Merrill has written a call for all of us to engage with our culture in a thoughtful and civil way. Our methods in seeking to influence society matter as well as our society aims. This book deserves a wide and sympathetic reading.

John Ortberg
Willow Creek Community Church

Dean Merrill has agonized over our declining culture for years and has been actively involved in a variety of responses. Now he has written cogently about his conclusions and experiences. Not everyone will agree with them, but Christians should certainly read him.

D. Stuart Briscoe
Elmbrook Church

SINNERS IN THE HANDS OF AN ANGRY CHURCH

Other Books by Dean Merrill

Fresh Wind, Fresh Fire (with Jim Cymbala)

Together at Home: A Proven Plan to Nurture Your Child's Faith and Spend Family Time (with Grace Merrill)

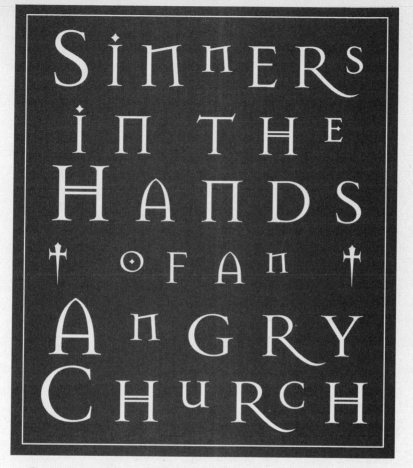

Sinners in the Hands of an Angry Church

FINDING A BETTER WAY TO INFLUENCE OUR CULTURE

Dean Merrill

ZondervanPublishingHouse
Grand Rapids, Michigan

A Division of HarperCollinsPublishers

Requests for information should be addressed to:

ZondervanPublishingHouse
Grand Rapids, Michigan 49530

Library of Congress Cataloging-in-Publication Data

Merrill, Dean.
    Sinners in the hands of an angry church : finding a better way to influence
our culture / Dean Merrill.
      p.   cm.
    Includes bibliographical references.
    ISBN: 0-310-21308-8
    1. Christianity and culture—United States—History—20th century. 2.
Christianity and politics—United States—History—20th century. 3. Com-
munication—Religious aspects—Christianity. 4. United States—Church
history—20th century. 5. United States—Moral conditions. 6. Evangelicalism
—United States—History—20th century. I. Title.
BR526.M47   1997
261'.0973—dc21
                                          97-23181
                                             CIP

Interior design by Sue Vandenberg Koppenol

Printed in the United States of America

---

97 98 99 00 01 02 03 04 /❖ DC/ 10 9 8 7 6 5 4 3 2 1

Contents

Part One

Fire and Rain

A contentious people will be a miserable people.

Jonathan Edwards
"Farewell Sermon," 1750

One

What Is God Thinking?

I have been pondering the message of this book for a long time—at least eight years. Its essence has come quietly, a bit now and a piece then, in reflective moments. But it has also arisen out of times of busyness and confusion. One such day was back in October 1992.

I left my office shortly after five o'clock that Thursday burdened with the latest evidences of a culture in moral decline. I had edited several articles for publication that spelled out the ongoing slippage. A presidential election loomed less than three weeks away, and at that point, conservative Christians were reluctantly starting to admit to each other, although not in public, that George Bush might go down in defeat for a second term in the White House.

If that happened, I realized, it would mark the first time in seven elections that the American evangelical community had not gotten what it wanted. All the way back to the chaotic campaign of 1968, Christians of a conservative bent had received their wishes: Richard Nixon over Hubert Humphrey, then Nixon again over George McGovern. In 1976 they were of mixed opinion, their Republican loyalties to Gerald Ford moderated somewhat by the "born-again" testimony of Jimmy Carter. Either man seemed acceptable. But by 1980 and 1984, the bumper stickers in most church parking lots strongly leaned toward Ronald Reagan. In 1988, George Bush was clearly the choice over Michael Dukakis. Six in a row. . . . But now the pro-choice Democrat from Arkansas was ahead in the polls. What would become of the cause of righteousness if Bill Clinton actually won the presidency?

Other battles pressed upon my mind as I pulled onto the freeway heading north: court decisions that week that made little sense, divorce statistics ballooning, government policies granting license to immoral behavior, Hollywood pumping out one visual cesspool after another. . . . What a wretched time to have to live!

In the weekly rhythm of our household, Thursday night meant choir rehearsal at church. My wife was the pianist; I was a member of the bass section. We ate a hurried meal and soon headed back south on the freeway, entering the building none too early for the seven o'clock practice.

Late October in our church has for a number of years been earmarked for a special event called "missions conference," a two-Sunday emphasis on world evangelism. Flags of the nations are strung on wires high across the sanctuary expanse, colorful posters are hung on the narthex walls, and members are asked to make "faith promises" to fund missions efforts in the coming months. It's a festive time, with video reports, theme-related music, and guest speakers from far corners of the world.

I remember two songs we practiced that Thursday night. Both were up-tempo, even energetic, supported not only by piano and synthesizer but also by a brass section, bass guitar, and drums. My fellow singers began to unleash the rhythm of ...

I could not help noticing the sharp contrast between the pessimism of my day at work and the buoyant optimism of the missions music.

> Look what God is doing
> All across the land!
> See His Spirit moving,
> Feel His mighty hand,
> Breaking chains of
>   darkness,
> Setting the captive free.
> Look what God is doing
> To those who do believe.
>
> Glory, hallelujah!
> Look what God is doing![1]

Ten minutes later the rehearsal had moved along to this chorus:

> There's going to be a revival in the land.
> There's going to be a revival in the land.
> From the north, from the south,
> From the east, from the west,
> There's going to be a revival in the land.[2]

Insight can indeed break through during the routine of a choir rehearsal. (I once read about a Minnesota engineer who, while fumbling to find the right pages in the music books that filled his lap, suddenly thought of a new use for the failed adhesive he had been trying to develop that day at the 3M Corporation—and thus was born our society's now ubiquitous self-sticking notes.) I could not help noticing the sharp contrast between the pessimism of my day at work and the buoyant optimism of the missions music. If I had stopped to sing anything during the day, it would have been *"There's going to be a disaster in the land"*—specifically in about three weeks, at the polls. Now here I was in the choir loft, my shoulders gently bobbing to the expectation of revival and God's blessing.

Was I kidding myself? Was all this just pep-rally music, designed merely to enthuse the congregation so they would open their checkbooks?

No, I had to admit, there were solid missions reports to back up the lyrics. God *was* doing amazing things in certain parts of the world. Scripture portions were being handed out by the millions in formerly Communist schools from Warsaw to Vladivostok. Latin Americans were packing soccer stadiums to hear the gospel preached. Drug users in North American cities were turning away from their addictions through the power of Christ. Orphans in Southeast Asia were being fed, cared for, educated, and loved in Jesus' name. *Look what God is doing. . . .*

As I left the church that evening, I was thoroughly confused. I didn't know what to feel. I was a walking case of what psychologists call *cognitive dissonance*, that state of mind when two parts of one's consciousness are in direct contradiction. "On the one hand. . . , but on the other hand. . . ," and you can't make the pieces mesh. All I knew was that I liked the choir outlook better than the office outlook. But was it credible? Was there indeed any basis for encouragement and hope in the run-up to Election Day?

In the grand scheme of things, of course, it didn't matter all that much what I did with my personal dilemma. More important for me—and for everyone else—was to grasp God's view of current reality. As he looked down from the vastness of heaven at this third planet from the sun, what was he seeing? What was he thinking? What was he saying to the angels about the goings-on here? What would he applaud, and what would he reproach? What did he wish his people to do—and not do?

PERSPECTIVE

Perspective is an elusive thing. Just when you

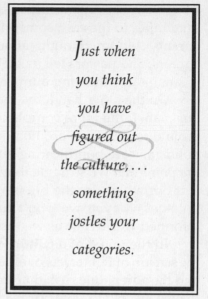

Just when you think you have figured out the culture, . . . something jostles your categories.

think you have grasped the big picture, you haven't. Just when you think you have figured out the culture and you know who's wearing white hats as opposed to who's wearing black hats, something jostles your categories. Hollywood turns out a decent, family-oriented movie for a change. *How did that happen?* you ask yourself. Congress votes to reinforce traditional marriage. *Where did that come from?* you wonder.

On the one hand, perspective ought to be easier than ever for our generation to maintain. We are the first to have those marvelous NASA photographs of the earth, a perfect sphere of blue and white, with a little brown dirt here and there, hanging majestically in the silent vastness of space. The pictures remind us that we are not so big after all. They also tell us that all five-and-a-half billion of us ride together on the same orb. If we choose not to get along, there are not a lot of alternative places to move.

We are better informed than any previous generation, thanks to CNN and all its media competitors. We know what life is like a thousand miles to the south and ten thousand miles to the east, something most of our great-grandparents seldom thought about. Pundits, commentators, authors, and pastors tell us their views of what modern life means, supplementing our personal observations.

On the other hand, the more the population grows on our planet, the more complex life becomes. Down here at ground level, horns are honking and TVs are blaring and politicians are pontificating and advocates are arguing, to the point that we struggle to integrate it all. It is difficult to sort out which are the big issues and which are the small potatoes. Maybe we don't have as much of a reliable, informed worldview as we thought.

In the midst of a culture war, the deafening rocketry, the scream of fighter jets overhead, the blue smoke in the air, and the adrenaline rush that urges us to press the attack (or maybe just try to save our necks) all converge to cloud the brain. Who can think straight with live ammunition zipping past the ears?

Something about all this reminds me of a passage in that great Russian epic *War and Peace* by Leo Tolstoy. The year is 1805, long before the days when combat became high-tech with radar screens and long-range missiles. Killing happens within a matter of yards; it is palpable, immediately human. You can see your enemy grimace as he falls to the blood-spattered earth.

Young Prince Andrey Bolkonsky and his comrades are struggling mightily to defend the motherland against Napoleon's invaders. On the morning of battle, as the fog lifts, the French suddenly begin showing up much closer than expected, catching the Russians and their Austrian allies off guard.

The battlefield erupts in clouds of smoke, guns blazing, men yelling, and horses charging. Prince Andrey urges his battalion forward. The French are so close that they try to wrestle cannons away from their handlers in order to wheel the machines around 180 degrees and start firing back at the Russians. Prince Andrey is figuring out what to do about this when something abruptly strikes him in the back of the head.

> "What's this? am I falling? my legs are giving way under me," he thought, and fell on his back. He opened his eyes. . . .Above him there was nothing but the sky—the lofty sky, not clear, but still immeasurably lofty, with grey clouds creeping quietly over it. "How quietly, peacefully, and triumphantly, and not like us running, shouting, and fighting. . .how differently are those clouds creeping over that lofty, limitless sky. How was it that I did not see that lofty sky before? And how happy I am to have found it at last. Yes! all is vanity, all is a cheat, except that infinite sky. There is nothing, nothing but that. . . .And thank God!"

The surging tide of pain builds up there on the hillside until Prince Andrey blacks out. He regains consciousness only in the cool of the evening, when the battle is over and the French have prevailed. The throb in his head tells him he is badly wounded.

Prince Andrey hears the sound of approaching hoof-beats and voices speaking French. None other than Napoleon himself is making a tour of the battlefield, relishing the scene of vanquished equipment and broken bodies. Andrey lies still.

> "That's a fine death!" said Napoleon, looking at Bolkonsky. . . . But he heard the words as he heard the buzzing of flies. . . . There was a burning pain in his head; he felt he was losing blood, and he saw above him the high, far-away, everlasting sky. . . . At that moment Napoleon seemed to him such a small, insignificant creature in comparison with what was passing now between his soul and that lofty, limitless sky with the clouds flying over it. . . . He moved his leg

faintly, and uttered a weak, sickly moan that touched himself. "Ah, he's alive," said Napoleon. "Pick up this young man and carry him to an ambulance!"[3]

As Andrey is lifted onto a stretcher, he blacks out again. But in the days that follow, as he is handed over to his own countrymen for recuperation, he cannot help thinking about the contrast of human battle overarched with eternal serenity, the vast firmament of the divine gazing down upon frenzied armies.

I wonder how this present culture war looks from the vantage point of the One "who sits in the heavens" (Ps. 2:4 NASB). How does he see our passions and protests, our campaigns and crusades? What is he thinking these days, these years?

We have no weekly letter from the throne to tell us, no overnight e-mail to advise us of God's view. But we do have a Book that describes his thinking about days gone by, which in some ways were more similar to our own time than is often assumed. From that record we can learn much.

Two

Scorching King Ahab

A cartoon lingers in my memory from the turbulent 1960s, when historic denominations began to speak out against societal ills. Ministers took to their pulpits to criticize the Vietnam War, racial injustice, male domination, capitalistic greed, police brutality, and other problems. Social commentary was largely the domain of liberals in those days; conservatives tended to keep quiet and support the status quo.

In this scene, a fiftyish couple is greeting the minister on their way out the church door after morning worship. The wife has a nice little hat on her head. The husband, a stuffy corporate-looking type, is not happy. He scowls as he says, "How come every Sunday you sound like one of those Old Testament guys?"

Indeed, the minister's sermons probably had carried a prophetic ring. He could have answered that he was but following an honorable tradition, proclaiming the Almighty's dismay at the behavior of evil human beings. After all, Isaiah had thundered such lines as

> *Woe to those who make unjust laws,*
>   *to those who issue oppressive decrees,*
> *to deprive the poor of their rights*
>   *and withhold justice from the oppressed of my people*
> *(Isa. 10:1–2).*

On that basis, shouldn't the clergy decry voting restrictions? Shouldn't they announce God's unhappiness with crooked politicians?

And what about Amos, who proclaimed,

> *For three sins of Israel,*
>   *even for four, I will not turn back my wrath.*
> *They sell the righteous for silver,*
>   *and the needy for a pair of sandals (Amos 2:6).*

The minister could draw a fairly straight line to modern sweatshops taking advantage of uneducated workers, or retailers in the ghetto jacking up prices to gouge customers who have no cars to go shopping elsewhere.

Today, strong critique is no longer the province of liberals alone. Conservative Christians, upset with political and legal trends as well as with degradation in movies, popular music, and television shows, have begun to "sound like Old Testament guys" too. In the face of high taxes, high abortion rates, removal of public references to God or the Scriptures, blatant pornography, and vigorous campaigns for homosexual acceptance, Christian leaders and laity are deeply concerned—and saying so. To quote only three of many:

It's time to say we must take back the schools. We've got to do something in America and take away the school system from the left-wing labor union and their left-wing cohorts that are destroying the moral fiber of the youth of America.[1]

An intense battle is being waged in this nation for the mind, soul and heart of *your* children and grand-children.
And frankly, *unless you act now you'll be on the los-ing side! . . .*
The cultural war is now targeting everything you hold dear as a responsible, God-fearing, freedom-lov-ing, pro-family American. And *the battle is at a critical stage.*
. . .The root cause of every one of America's prob-lems lies in the breakdown of the two-parent, tradi-tional family.[2]

If God's judgment befalls wicked nations as well as disobedient individuals, . . .how can our own coun-try escape His wrath? . . .We have forgotten the moral and spiritual principles with which we began, and now we stand. . .at the most important crossroads in our his-tory. One road leads to continued rebellion and defi-ance of the Holy One of Israel. Traveling further down that slippery slope will lead, I believe, to the destruc-tion of the social order as we have known it.[3]

No doubt God is indeed displeased with America at the turn of the millennium. Whenever innocent people suf-fer, whenever sin triumphs, whenever his plan and his Son are scorned, he cannot help being saddened. This is not the world, or the nation, as he wants it to be.

TELLING IT STRAIGHT

In Old Testament times, God seemed to say exactly what he thought of cultural wickedness. He made himself abun-dantly clear on such issues as idolatry, lust, and mistreating the poor. Whenever his chosen people, the nation of Israel, strayed from their covenant with him, he quickly and articulately spoke through his prophets to point out the problem.

Have you ever stopped to notice that the books of just the writing prophets (Isaiah through Malachi)—which are at least 90 percent corrective in nature—take up as much space in the Bible as the whole New Testament? We get equal doses of Jeremiah and Paul (sixty-nine pages each in my Bible). We get as much Ezekiel as John. We get more Micah than James, more Zechariah than the great apostle Peter. And this doesn't even take into account the nonwriting seers, from Ahijah to Elisha to Huldah the prophetess, who scolded the wayward Israelites verbally but left no trail of parchment.

Perhaps the most vivid face-off occurred in the 860s and 850s B.C., when the northern kingdom of Israel was ruled by a contemptible buffoon named Ahab and his scheming wife, Jezebel. Any thought of being faithful leaders of the people of God was long gone. Idol shrines, including Asherah poles—grotesque, oversized wooden phalluses—suddenly appeared everywhere. "Ahab son of Omri did more evil in the eyes of the LORD than any of those before him," says 1 Kings 16:30. "He ... considered it trivial to commit the sins of Jeroboam son of Nebat ... and began to serve Baal and worship him" (v. 31).

His aggressive wife was adept at bullying the clergy (1 Kings 18:4; 19:1–2) as well as organizing kangaroo court trials (1 Kings 21:7–15) to get what she wanted. At the end of her life, after her husband's death, she was still so hated by her own staff that they didn't mind pitching her out of an upstairs window the minute the opportunity presented itself. Stray dogs devoured her body (2 Kings 9:30–37). Can we imagine worse leadership? Can we think of more repugnant role models for a nation?

God responded to Ahab's provocation by sending a wild man stomping into Ahab's court with a bold warning of drought. God would not tolerate the evil promoted by Ahab's court, Elijah announced. Judgment was on its way.

That visit led, as every Sunday school pupil knows, to the dramatic showdown three years later on Mount Carmel. The king snarled something about Elijah being a "troubler of Israel." The

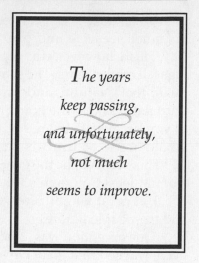

The years keep passing, and unfortunately, not much seems to improve.

prophet shot back, "I have not made trouble for Israel. But you and your father's family have. You have abandoned the LORD's commands and have followed the Baals" (1 Kings 18:17–18). Before the end of the day, more than words had been exchanged. God had proved his power with a dramatic rush of fire.

But Ahab was not impressed. Throughout his remaining years, he talked with various prophets, played mental games with them, but never yielded to the Lord they served. He died pursuing an enemy the Lord's spokesman had advised him to leave alone (1 Kings 22). Ahab's name became an ongoing icon for evil; if you wanted to say something bad about a person, you could say that he "walked in the ways of the house of Ahab" (e.g., 2 Chron. 22:3), and everyone knew what you meant.

THE SINNERS AREN'T LISTENING

It all sounds familiar, doesn't it? A nation in moral decline, outrageous things happening on the streets every day, a government making the problems worse rather than trying to solve them, and God-fearing voices trying desperately to turn the tide. The years keep passing, and unfortunately, not much seems to improve.

Elijah, however, was not the only prophet whose warnings fell on deaf ears. The same could be said of Hosea, Jeremiah, Joel, Nahum, and especially Ezekiel, to whom the Lord flatly said, "The house of Israel is not willing to listen to you because they are not willing to listen to me, for the whole house of Israel is hardened and obstinate" (Ezek. 3:7).This seems to be the general rule throughout the period from at least Solomon's time through the Exile. Prophets speak at great length, often with eloquence and passion—and the people ignore.

One exception was Jonah. He went (eventually) to Nineveh, warned that great city of God's impending judgment for their wickedness, and got a positive response. A spirit of repentance swept over the population, from the vendors in the street to the king on the throne. Revival took place. Even Jesus saluted this awakening and chided his own generation for not responding likewise (Matt. 12:41).

Nineveh's revival didn't last forever, of course. By the time Nahum prophesied a century or more later, Nineveh was back to its old corruption. But let the record show that at least one Old Testament prophet (and a shaky one at that) was indeed listened to. The rest, however, including men with far more spiritual character than Jonah, went to their graves with little to show for their efforts.

In our time, we have mounted major endeavors to turn the United States back to God. We have preached, prodded, and protested. We have exhorted presidents, senators, governors, and mayors to honor the Lord and pass laws reflecting biblical morality. We have signed petitions and written scathing letters to the editor. We have flooded telephone switchboards. We have warned political candidates that if they offend Christian sensibilities, they will pay a heavy price at the polls. Sometimes we have been able to deliver on our threats, sometimes not.

Meanwhile, is the country becoming more righteous? Are the streets less violent? Is drug use declining? Are national leaders more respectful of the church and morality?

The answers are painfully obvious.

In drawing the analogy with Old Testament times, I do not mean to imply that the prophets should not have done what they did. God told them

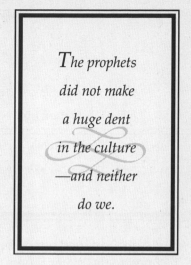

The prophets did not make a huge dent in the culture —and neither do we.

to speak, and they obeyed. Enduring cold stares and even physical assault (remember Jeremiah's trip to the pit?), they relayed the divine message in spite of rejection. It is not for us to question what God directed the prophets to do. At the very least, we learn today from their writings how seriously God hates sin, especially among people who claim to be his own. And their writings do also include occasional words of hope and comfort as well as predictions of the coming Messiah. I am only commenting on the *effectiveness* of their words in changing the primary audience's behavior. For all their intensity, the prophets did not make a huge dent in the culture—and neither do we. Sinners back then did not listen very well, and they are not listening very well today.

BACKFIRE

At times our well-meaning efforts antagonize the people we wish to influence, producing the opposite result of what we wanted. Larry Poland, a Christian who has labored at least fifteen years inside the Hollywood community starting Bible studies and encouraging more responsible programming, tells how NBC decided a few years back that a certain

> *At times*
>
> *our well-meaning*
>
> *efforts antagonize*
>
> *the people we wish*
>
> *to influence.*

Saturday Night Live actor needed to be disciplined for vulgarity. (While some Americans may think that television has no standards these days and that anything goes, the networks do in fact have internal guidelines for what may not be said on the air.) This particular actor kept crossing the line, and because the show was aired live, his words could not be edited out or rerecorded; they were immediately beamed to the living rooms of America. He was warned several times to stop his vulgarity, but he would not. Finally, the network decided to fire him.

But just then, thousands of cards and letters began arriving at NBC headquarters from Christian activists demanding that something be done. The mail had been triggered by a conservative Christian group that had sent out an indignant letter that called for protest. To NBC, the whole case now changed color. If they fired the actor, they would appear to be caving in to the religious right. The vice presidents met, discussed the problem from all sides, and elected to sit tight. The final result was that the comedian got to keep his job after all.

Something went awry here—something that illustrates the shortcomings of head-on confrontation. People—especially powerful people—do not like to be pushed to do something they didn't think of first. They will find a way to save face and their sense of independence if at all possible.

Young children can be intimidated into changing their behavior because a very tall grown-up gets noisy and says, "Do as I say, or else." But adults are a different matter altogether. They usually weigh the pros and cons, then act out of their own self-interest. Their internal values soon float to the surface.

That is why a "culture war" model has its limitations. Head-on confrontation is external; it doesn't make the opponents *want* to change. If they react, it is out of fear, which soon wears off. Others are too self-assured or too stubborn to bend at all. Their pride makes them hold the line regardless of the merits of the argument.

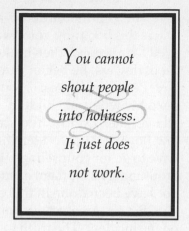

You cannot shout people into holiness. It just does not work.

Eugene H. Peterson tells a wonderful story about taking his wife and three children to visit Yellowstone National Park.[4] Having grown up in nearby Montana, Peterson has always carried a fervent love for nature, the open sky, the wide world God made. As a boy, he attended a grade school named for Cornelius Hedges, the lawyer who got President Teddy Roosevelt interested in preserving this park against chainsaws and bulldozers forever. Eugene and his wife raised their children with the Sierra Club motto "Take nothing but pictures, leave nothing but footprints," to the point that it was almost considered Holy Writ.

On this particular day, while walking through a mountain meadow, the family suddenly spotted a little boy of only four or five years doing the most horrible deed: picking fringed gentians! He kept snatching the exquisite alpine flowers, one after another, filling his chubby little fist. Not only was this destructive, but it is also against the law to pick any flower in a national park.

The boy was maybe thirty yards away. Eugene was outraged. This had to be stopped—immediately. He cupped his hands to his mouth and bellowed, "HEY! STOP THAT! DON'T PICK THE FLOWERS! IT'S ILLEGAL!"

The child shuddered as his head snapped up to see where this booming voice was coming from. He stood wide-eyed for a second, then broke into tears. Dropping his handful of flowers, he began running for cover.

Peterson writes: "You can imagine what happened next. My wife and children—my children especially—were all over me. 'Daddy! You scared him! He was just picking a few flowers, and you terrified him. He's probably going to have to go for counseling when he's forty years old.'" A vigorous family argument ensued about what should or should not have been done in this case.

But the greatest wisdom emerged as Peterson reflected on the incident. The truth to be learned from the interchange in the meadow, he realized, was this: *You cannot shout people into holiness.* It just does not work. You may win a momentary stoppage of whatever evil you were attacking. You may get people to conform to your wishes temporarily, but the result will not last. And meanwhile, all other kinds of damage will have been done.

The Old Testament-like strategy of scorching the King Ahabs and the flower pickers of our time, at least as we have been practicing it in the last few decades, is not producing the outcomes we seek. There must be a better way.

Three

Blessings for the Honorable Nero

I don't mean to be disrespectful, but I do believe it is fair to say that when the Son of God showed up on this planet and began to minister to people, he triggered mass confusion. After all, he had no ties to the Jerusalem establishment. He lacked a rabbinical education. He wasn't from the priestly tribe of Levi. He had the nerve to declare openly more than once, "Moses said, . . . but I say, . . ." He challenged everything from Sabbath protocol to temple fund-raising.

People scratched their heads and tried to find an appropriate category for him. Troublemaker? Guru? Populist? Rebel? Egoist? Crusader? Son of Beelzebub? Yes, but . . . well, no . . . on the other hand—back and forth they went in their minds. He didn't quite fit any one box.

He's not changing governments.... He's changing people.

The whole New Testament is an experience in paradigm shift. What Jesus came to be and say and do collided sharply with past assumptions. He spoke of an invisible kingdom, whereas the Jews had labored mightily for centuries to build and then rebuild a tangible nation. He taught that people didn't need to seek revenge or settle old scores after all; they could forgive and walk away. He criticized sin but mainly among the religiously inclined; he was strangely quiet about the sins of the Roman occupation troops and of the caravan traders who came through.

In a musical play about the life of Christ entitled *The Choice,* a handsome young Roman centurion named Marcus, who's single, takes notice of a somewhat spunky Jewish maiden named Hannah. While both guard themselves against falling headlong in love, they enjoy talking to each other and matching wits. One day Hannah coaxes Marcus into going along to hear the itinerant from Nazareth, who is speaking on a nearby hillside.

On the way, they get into a brief argument about whether Roman justice is fair and what role a Messiah might play in Israel's political future. Then, in one of the most insightful lines of the play, Hannah says, "I don't pretend to be wise ... but I do know that Jesus is special. He's different. He's not changing governments, Marcus. He's changing *people.*"[1]

Indeed he was. Jesus was in the business of cleaning up society one person at a time, from the inside. He held out little hope for reforming societal systems or getting pagans to behave themselves better through public pressure. He called for a revolution of the heart, which in turn would make all the difference in visible conduct. Somehow he thought this was more effective in the long run.

THE ULTIMATE TEST

Eventually Jesus' views were brought to a painfully personal level when he was arrested and thrown into the gears of a manifestly corrupt legal system. Pilate began to cross-examine him, and the interchange quickly went off track. This suspect did not beg for his life, defend his honor, engage in name-dropping, or do any of the usual things a man on trial would do. When Pilate wondered aloud what was really going on here, Jesus replied, "My kingdom is not of this world. If it were, my servants would fight to prevent my arrest by the Jews. But now my kingdom is from another place" (John 18:36).

Why not fight? Why not protest the flagrant lack of due process under the law? Why shouldn't Jesus' disciples push every lever within their reach to save the neck of their innocent leader? Because his kingdom was not of this world. His whole operating system came from "another place." His movement did not play by the world's rules. He had taught the futility of fighting to gain earthly advantage. A few hours earlier in the garden, a disciple had temporarily forgotten that lesson and pulled out his sword. Jesus sharply rebuked him: "No more of this!" (Luke 22:51).

William Law was a remarkable English devotional writer of the 1700s. In commenting on Jesus' statement to Pilate, he noted that Jesus' kingdom "was so different in kind, and so superior in nature to any kingdom of this world, that no sort of worldly power could either help or hinder it." In other words, what God had in mind didn't need the tender mercies of Rome (or Washington, or Ottawa). Nor could any capital stymie his work in the long run. William Law continued: "And what more could professing Christians do to show that they are not yet in that true heavenly kingdom than to set about to build their own kingdoms of strife?"[2] What more, indeed?

Years later one of Jesus' close followers explained, "When they hurled their insults at him, he did not retaliate; when he suffered, he made no threats. Instead, he entrusted himself to him who judges justly" (1 Peter 2:23). Certainly Pontius Pilate was not apt to judge justly, but then Pontius Pilate was not the ultimate referee. The viewpoint of the heavenly Judge would prevail in the end.

We must not dismiss this behavior by Jesus as a special one-time case due to the fact that the world's redemption through death on the cross was at stake. While that is true, the mind-set of Jesus before Pilate is entirely consistent with the rest of his life. It is also what the apostles took with them once he ascended and they went forth to impact the first-century world for God.

THE "LITTLE BOOT"

For sake of illustration, let us look at two periods during the time of the book of Acts. In both cases, note how the apostles responded to a decadent, crooked society.

The first time period is A.D. 37–41, or roughly the last part of Acts 9 through most of Acts 11. Here the newly converted Saul is introduced to the Jerusalem church as friend rather than foe. The apostle Peter brings healing and even resurrection power to the towns of Lydda and Joppa. He is then nudged across ethnic lines to proclaim the Good News in Cornelius's house—and has to explain to his colleagues back in Jerusalem why he did so. Finally, an anonymous group of pioneers establish a new church in Antioch, which grows so marvelously that Barnabas makes a trip to check it out. These are wonderful years of advance for the gospel on a variety of fronts. Because no epistles were written during these still-early years, only by the Acts reports do we know what the apostles were doing and thinking.

Meanwhile, what was happening on the political front? What kind of leader presided over the Roman Empire, of which Jerusalem, Joppa, and Antioch were a part?

The emperor's name was Caligula, "the little boot," a general's son who came to the throne at the brash age of twenty-five. History tells us he was a brutal tyrant who raised taxes, spent prodigious amounts of money, and murdered the prefect who had helped him get chosen as emperor in the first place. He shocked the Roman senate by announcing that he intended to appoint a new member to that august body: his horse!

In his sexual life, there were no boundaries; Caligula enjoyed the intimacy of both women and men. He was particularly smitten with his three sisters, especially Drusilla, even though she was married to someone else—whom he ordered to be executed. People seriously thought the young ruler was mentally ill.

Caligula's outrages were not confined to Rome. There were ugly incidents in Alexandria and also in Palestine, culminating with his order to have a statue of himself erected in the Jerusalem temple. Herod Agrippa (the regional king, mentioned in Acts 12) convinced him that maybe that wasn't such a wise idea, given Jewish sensibilities, and he backed down. But the Roman world by then was fed up with Caligula. The military murdered him at a sports event on January 24, A.D. 41, at which time he was only in his late twenties.

What did the early Christians think of Caligula's conduct? They must have been appalled like everyone else. Did they write letters of protest? Did Peter go back to his newly converted friend Cornelius and say, "Can't you do something about this crazy emperor? I'm only a Jew, but you're part of the Roman military. You have connections. As a Spirit-filled Christian now, you need to use your clout for the defense of righteousness and public decency. What action are you going to take?" The book of Acts is completely silent. Whatever the early believers thought and did about Caligula's disgraceful antics, it wasn't considered significant enough to make it into Luke's history.

WILD MAN ON THE LOOSE

The next emperor was Caligula's uncle, Claudius I, mentioned in Acts 11:28 as well as in 18:2. He was generally competent during his thirteen-year reign, although he did have a few troubles at home: His second wife poisoned him in the end. That set up her son (but not his) to be the next Caesar, a sixteen-year-old boy named Nero.

This brings us to our second case study, A.D. 54–68, which starts about the time of Acts 19 and runs through the rest of the book and beyond. Paul finishes his third missionary journey, heads for Jerusalem, gets arrested, languishes in local prisons for a couple of years, finally appeals to the "supreme court" of this day—Nero's court—and takes a very rough ride across the Mediterranean toward Rome.

These are the years that give us the vast majority of Paul's epistles—probably all of them except Galatians and the two Thessalonians, written earlier. These are also the years when Peter wrote (or dictated) his first letter; and perhaps the book of James was sent out in the early part of this period as well. We have a wealth of history and correspondence to give us the tenor of early-church thinking.

Nero started things off with a bang by poisoning his fourteen-year-old stepbrother. (Like mother, like son, apparently.) He carried on a couple of very public affairs. In time he had his ambitious mother murdered. He got married but then had his first wife murdered as well.

His erstwhile tutor, the wise philosopher Seneca, who had been trying to keep a lid on the young man, eventually threw up his hands in dismay. Nero was known for cavorting in the streets of Rome at all hours of the night and early

morning. He loved to race chariots and also fancied himself a
great actor; the theater crowds
obligingly applauded even as
they winced at his lack of talent.

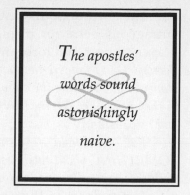

The apostles' words sound astonishingly naive.

As everyone knows, when
Rome went up in flames in A.D.
64, Nero pointed to the Christians as a handy scapegoat,
which unleashed vicious perse-
cution. It is generally believed
that both Peter and Paul lost their lives around this time.

Meanwhile, Nero ran the empire into serious debt; his
gifts to various friends each year mounted up to five times
the cost of maintaining the whole Roman army. When the
senate finally began laying groundwork to impeach him,
Nero, then thirty years old, avoided further embarrassment
by slitting his own throat. He left the treasury bankrupt and
the soldiers well behind in their pay.

Again, how did the early Christians react to Nero's
conduct? What was their view of an immature, immoral,
ruthless megalomaniac at the head of their government?

Listen to Paul: "I urge, then, . . . that requests, prayers,
intercession and *thanksgiving* be made for everyone—for
kings and all those in authority. . . . This is good, and pleases
God our Savior, who wants all men to be saved and to come
to a knowledge of the truth" (1 Tim. 2:1–4, italics added).

Listen to Peter: "It is God's will that by doing good you
should silence the ignorant talk of foolish men. . . . Show
proper respect for everyone: Love the brotherhood of believers, fear God, honor the king" (1 Peter 2:15, 17).

Listen to James: "Be patient, then, brothers, until the
Lord's coming. See how the farmer waits for the land to
yield its valuable crop. . . . You too, be patient and stand firm,
because the Lord's coming is near. Don't grumble" (James
5:7–9).

Their words sound astonishingly naive. In the face of outrageous behavior in high places, they calmly talk of prayer, respect, and forbearance. *What is wrong with you gentlemen? Don't you see the moral collapse? Aren't you outraged? How can you tolerate the ongoing abuse of power, the flagrant sin in the imperial court, the disgusting offense against all propriety and responsibility?*

Paul, you hold the privilege of Roman citizenship; DO SOMETHING about this! Rise up! Launch a popular protest that will force this evil monster from the throne.

Listen again to the rugged fisherman: "Do not repay evil with evil or insult with insult, but with blessing, because to this you were called" (1 Peter 3:9).

Hear the perspective of the one-time Pharisee activist: "Get rid of all bitterness, rage and anger, brawling and slander, along with every form of malice" (Eph. 4:31). "For our struggle is not against flesh and blood, but against. . .the spiritual forces of evil in the heavenly realms" (Eph. 6:12).

Christian people and groups in our time are engaged in titanic struggles against flesh and blood. The enemies are clearly named, along with their phone numbers, addresses, fax numbers, and photographs. If only Governor So-and-So could be removed, if only Senator Such-and-Such could be defeated, if only this cabinet secretary or that federal administrator could be censured by popular outcry, the tide of infamy would be reversed.

Paul and the other apostles seem to stand quietly by, wishing we would realize who the real enemies are. They are not flesh-and-blood creatures, however misguided. The real enemies are Satan and his minions, who have won over the minds and values of many who temporarily hold governmental power. That is not to say anything insulting about those particular politicians; they are fallen creatures like millions of others in the world. Rather, it is to say that we will get a lot further if we focus on the true fountainhead of all sin and rebellion against God. And he doesn't live on Pennsylvania Avenue.

Were the apostles spineless and laissez-faire with regard to *all* things perverse? Did they lack the moral fortitude to call sin by its proper name across the board? Not at all. Paul is famous for his vice lists —to quote just one, "sexual immorality, impurity and debauchery; idolatry and witchcraft; hatred, discord, jealousy, fits of rage, selfish ambition, dissensions, factions and envy; drunkenness, orgies, and the like. I warn you, as I did before, that those who live like this will not inherit the kingdom of God" (Gal. 5:19–21). He shows no hesitation in naming sins and outlining their consequences.

> *We will get a lot further if we focus on the true fountainhead of all sin and rebellion against God. And he doesn't live on Pennsylvania Avenue.*

But neither does Paul expect people such as Nero to straighten up and live virtuously on their own. The only hope for people who are "dead in trespasses and sins" (Eph. 2:1 KJV) is to experience a new birth and come "alive with Christ" (v. 5 NIV). Thus, Paul urges the churches, in the 1 Timothy passage quoted above, to pray for everyone's salvation—even the playboy emperor's. That is the kind of transformation, Paul taught, that would finally do some good.

"BUT DEMOCRACY IS DIFFERENT"

Some will say that maybe the apostolic writers didn't really know what was going on in Nero's administration. After all, they didn't have an ambitious press corps reporting all the juicy details by satellite on the six o'clock news.

Not all that much has changed since A.D. 68.

However, news did travel throughout the empire—just not as fast. And Peter and Paul especially did a great deal of traveling. They met many kinds of people in many provinces. Both eventually ended up in Rome itself. The letters of Ephesians, Philippians, Colossians, 2 Timothy, Philemon, and 1 Peter were no doubt written in that very city. The apostolic writers were not in the dark.

Others will quickly argue that life and citizenship in the Roman world was not the same as in today's modern democracies, with our governance "of the people, by the people, for the people." That is true. The early Christians, Jews, Greeks, Egyptians, and others in the empire had no access to the ballot box. The levers of power were reserved for a privileged few. Nevertheless, the power of the masses was still a force to be reckoned with. If one abused the populace too much, they could make life difficult. History is full of the stories of Jewish resistance to Roman rule, for example. Ordinary people in other parts of the empire staged their own protests.

Beyond this reality, we must not assume that the tone of the New Testament epistles is merely utilitarian—that Paul and Peter were trying to keep the Christians calm just to stay out of harm's way. These were courageous men filled with the power of the Holy Spirit. They hardly cowered in the face of imperial force. Instead, their teaching was inspired by the Spirit to guide Christians of all centuries, under all regimes. Their words must not be discounted as relevant only "back then."

The early Christians saw themselves the way Jesus had taught them to see: as hope and light in the midst of a vast sea of spiritual darkness. They knew they were a minority group, but that troubled them not in the least. Their calling was to represent Christ with honor and dignity, come what may, "in a crooked and depraved generation, in which you shine like stars in the universe as you hold out the word of life" (Phil. 2:15–16). Paul's picture says it well: an inky sky punctured only occasionally by a bright star here, another star there, another over there, signaling hope and warmth in the cultural nighttime. It is a picture we would do well to ponder today. Not all that much has changed since A.D. 68.

A DIFFERENT APPROACH: THE ZEALOTS

There was, I should mention, an alternate view in the first century on what to do with the nasty Romans. A resistance movement referred to as the Zealots was formed not long after Jesus was born. Its members fervently believed that something had to be done; they couldn't just sit by and wait for Caesar's troops to go home. They had to put pressure on them, make life difficult for them, raise the cost of their occupation whenever and wherever they could.

One of Jesus' twelve disciples had ties to this movement; both Luke 6:15 and Acts 1:13 refer to him as "Simon the Zealot."

In the last few years of Nero's reign, as Nero's behavior became more obnoxious than ever, the Zealots decided it was time for major action. They led the guerrilla resistance in Jerusalem starting around A.D. 66 that eventually brought a new Roman general, Titus, to the scene. His bloody destruction of the Holy City in A.D. 70, when the temple was burned to the ground, broke the back of the Jewish people—and helped enhance Titus's resume toward becoming emperor nine years later.

The Zealots did not entirely give up, however. Those who escaped the holocaust holed up in a rugged fortress called Masada along the Dead Sea. There, 960 of them lasted until A.D. 73, when 15,000 Roman troops finally came to mop up for good. One awful night, the Zealots committed mass suicide rather than surrender.

The Zealots were the activists of their time, deeply patriotic and fervent in defense of the Torah, the Law of God. Much pain and suffering followed in their wake, however, not only among their own ranks but among bystanders as well. In the end, their crusade failed; the pagans were aroused enough to muster overwhelming force and rule the land with an iron fist.

Thus the Zealots teach us that protest has its limitations. Frontal resistance to evil regimes does not always win the day. The view of the first-century church was rather to trust in the All-Powerful One and shed his light upon the hearts and minds of those who have not yet taken him seriously.

The last book of the New Testament, John's Revelation, casts one last ray of thought on the issue. Written after much of the dust had settled—certainly after the blood of the last Zealot had dried on the rocks—it portrays good versus evil in cosmic terms.

In a prelude of sorts, chapters 2 and 3 provide the words of the risen Lord to churches under fire. The first message, to Ephesus, shows a congregation gritting its teeth against bad influences:

"I know that you cannot tolerate wicked men" (2:2).

"You have tested those who claim to be apostles but are not, and have found them false" (v. 2).

"You hate the practices of the Nicolaitans" (v. 6). (The Nicolaitans were a compromising group that waffled in the face of paganism, particularly when it came to sexual matters. A little "flexibility" of the rules was fine with them.)

The Ephesian church stood tough. They were vigilant, aggressive in rooting out evil. No compromise for them.

Yet they were in danger of losing their "lampstand" altogether! The lampstand, according to Revelation 1:20, symbolized the church itself. Jesus told them in no uncertain terms that despite their unbending stands for righteousness, their entire fellowship was about to topple. Why? Because of the loss of love, the loss of spiritual freshness as in earlier years.

We can stand for purity and holiness all we want, but without the life of the Spirit energizing us and bringing warmth and goodness to our souls and relationships, we are in jeopardy.

At the very end of the book of Revelation, after John has watched torrents of evil, plagues, fire, smoke, fearsome beasts, hail, burning sulfur, and all the rest—he collapses at an angel's feet. He can take no more. What is he to think or do about all this mess in the world?

The angel gives a closing word of perspective: "Let him who does wrong continue to do wrong; let him who is vile continue to be vile" (22:11). In other words, we will not stop wrongdoers by external pressure. Their inner vileness will come out regardless. But in the meantime, the angel continues, "let him who does right continue to do right; and let him who is holy continue to be holy."

Notice the verbs: "does. . .is; does. . .is." The things people *do* spring out of what and who they *are* on the inside. The key to changing their value system and improving the world's condition is nothing less than the life-changing power of the gospel of Jesus Christ. Once this power is brought to bear on the unconverted soul, the ripple effect touches all matters of personal morality and opinions on public policy. That is why C. S. Lewis, perhaps the most brilliant Christian mind of the twentieth century, could write, "He who converts his neighbour has performed the most practical Christian-political act of all."[3]

Four

The Christian Stance in a Fallen Society

One of the reasons the New Testament view is so relevant to us is that, in North America today, people who take God seriously are in fact a minority group just as they were in the Roman Empire.

Think about the numbers for a moment. On any given weekend, about 37 percent of Americans show up in church. The other 63 percent are reading the paper, making love, drinking coffee, sleeping in, playing golf, or engaging in some other form of recreation. Church attendance, I freely admit, is no accurate gauge of the condition of the soul, but it is a place to start. It is a far better indicator than, say, the fact that 82 percent tell pollsters they're "religious" or 96 percent "believe in

God." If they can't be bothered even to attend church, their spiritual sentiments must not run very deep.

Of the 37 percent in the pews, how many are there for truly godly reasons? How many are serious about Christ being their Lord, their authority in daily life? Again, there is no way to measure, but let's be generous and say that two-thirds (or 25 percent of the whole population) are indeed intentional *Christ-followers,* to use Bill Hybels's term. (The Chicago megachurch pastor coined this phrase as an alternate to *Christians,* a label that can mean just about anything—or nothing—these days.)

Who are the other churchgoers? They are decent people who show up on Sunday out of cultural heritage, or to please their spouse, or to set a good example for the kids, or to make business contacts, or to meet members of the opposite sex, or for any number of other motives. They may be formal members and even office holders in the churchly institution. But their presence is not a sign of spiritual commitment.

Twenty-five percent of the population, ladies and gentlemen, does not a majority make. (Neither does 37 percent.) While those Americans who are serious about their faith may comprise a larger percentage than in any other society on earth, they are still only about a fourth. And that estimate, as I said, is probably generous. George Gallup Jr. says in his 1992 book *The Saints Among Us* that while many citizens are religious in a loose sense, the core U.S. population living deeply religious lives amounts to only about 13 percent.[1]

What we have in America today is a *Christ-Following Minority*—and an *Independent Majority* at least three times as large. By "independent" I mean they are beholden to no particular authority other than themselves. These people are self-managed, going through life just as the Israelites did

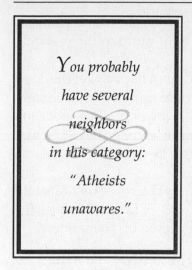

You probably have several neighbors in this category: "Atheists unawares."

long ago in the time of the judges, when "everyone did as he saw fit" (Judg. 21:25).

Sometimes the Independent Majority behaves itself better than at other times. Trends rise and fall. Crime rates ebb and flow. At this moment in history it seems that behavior is generally slipping. But the governing factor is the same as it always has been: These people do what they feel like doing, constrained only by what they sense to be in their self-interest.

To use the familiar Campus Crusade for Christ drawing made famous in the "Four Spiritual Laws" booklet, these are people whose internal throne is occupied by "I." Some of them are very nice and many of them are very bright. You probably have several neighbors in this category. They say hello at the mailbox and might even loan you a snow shovel if you needed it, but they are still independently controlled. An academic friend of mine refers to them as "atheists unawares." Only a quarter of Americans can be said to have placed Christ on the throne of their lives. And even in these cases, the Master frequently gets bumped around.

Thus, it is no wonder that when researchers ask the American public a question such as "Is abortion murder?" more people say yes than no—but then hesitate to say the government should do much to stop it. Their moral muddle is abundantly evident. A CBS/*New York Times* poll found a vote of 48 percent to 40 percent in agreement that abortion is murder (the other 12 percent couldn't make up their minds), while a *Los Angeles Times* poll the same year was even more decisive: 58 percent yes, 34 percent no, 8 percent unclear.

But should the practice be proscribed by law? Nah, not really. A little murder here, a little murder there—well, whatever.

Talk about confusion! One cannot hope to get this kind of society to consistently do the right thing or vote the right way. The populace is hopelessly incoherent. If the abortion question, or any similar moral issue, were put to a popular referendum, the result would likely be anything but logical, let alone biblical.

So it goes in a fallen society. As the *hrossa* on Mars told Ransom more than once in one of C. S. Lewis's science fiction novels, ours is the planet inhabited by "bent ones."[2]

AS GOOD AS WE WANNA THINK WE ARE

But of course, Americans do not think they are illogical, immoral, or confused. James Davison Hunter, a sociology professor at the University of Virginia, says at the very start of one of his books, "We Americans generally want to think of ourselves as good people. That, in many respects, is where the trouble begins."[3]

The assumption that we are all pretty decent people has received much applause over the decades. It got off to a very strong start at the beginning of our nation, with the founding fathers' high regard for Enlightenment-style reason and the nobility of man (a matter we shall explore further in chapter 6). More recently the preachments of humanism have placed the individual on a high pedestal. In a 1991 survey by George Barna, 83 percent of Americans agreed with the statement "People are basically good."[4] Christians, however, know that "nothing good lives in me, that is, in my sinful nature." Like Paul, millions of North Americans "have the desire to do what is good, but. . .cannot carry it out" (Rom. 7:18). For evidence of this fact, read any daily newspaper.

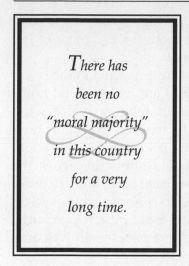

There has been no "moral majority" in this country for a very long time.

The Christ-Following Minority has no choice but to understand the present reality. There *is* no "moral majority" in this country; there hasn't been for a very long time. For instance, did you know that in the 1760s, just a few years before the American Revolution, one out of every three babies was conceived out of wedlock? Of course, their mothers usually covered things up by quickly getting married so that only one out of fifteen babies had no official father at birth.[5] But the fact remains: Premarital sex was alive and booming back then just as it is now. To pretend that there is a moral consensus today in our country, with evangelical Christians setting the pace—and then getting upset when evil prevails at the box office, in the legislature, before the high courts, or on the magazine stand—is to live in a dream world. What did we realistically expect?

Our fantasy leads us to suffer the same kind of dislocation as that experienced in recent years by the white minority in the Republic of South Africa. Though vastly outnumbered by other ethnic groups, whites have historically felt they should be in charge of the country. That day, however, is past. The majority has now taken over, and there has been little choice but to work out a rapprochement.

"But Christians *shouldn't* have to fight for basic morality in their own country!" some cry in frustration. "This whole situation is wrong." Welcome to the real world. This is not the Garden of Eden. It's not even next door.

Richard J. Mouw, president of Fuller Theological Seminary, writes, "Seeing ourselves as a *remnant* does not sit comfortably with today's prospering, upwardly mobile evangelicals."[6] But a remnant, a modest-sized piece of the whole, is what we are, like it or not.

Philip Yancey tells about a Muslim acquaintance who made a striking comment: "In the Qur'an, I can find nothing to teach us how to be a minority religion, while in the New Testament I can find nothing to teach Christians how to be a majority religion."[7] What a fascinating observation! The Muslim motif, he says, is to come thundering across the desert in a cloud of sand and dominate everything in one's path. The Christian motif, in sharp contrast, aspires to no such conquest. It rather aspires to work quietly inside the human heart—an activity that some people will welcome and more will not.

HOW DOES A MINORITY BEHAVE?

Four reactions to minority status are possible, and we see all four being practiced among Christians today.[8]

1. *Anxiousness.* There is an abundance of hand-wringing in the land. "Did you hear what the Supreme Court did now? Isn't it terrible? I just don't know what's going to become of this country before long."

Others believe they do know what is going to become of us. "We're headed right down the drain as a nation," they predict. "This society is so rotten that we won't last another thirty years."

Polls have shown that Americans are currently doing a lot of worrying. Even good news from the stock market or the medical scene is written off as a blip on the screen that cannot last. The days ahead are definitely going to be darker, people say.

Sometimes anxiety-ridden Christians will paper over this reaction with a closing cliché about divine superiority. For example, "But you know, God's still on the throne...." How that remark connects to the preceding ones is never quite clear. People go on fretting about a world they believe is washing away from underneath their feet, soon to pitch them into overpowering waters.

2. *Apathy.* This reaction is related to the first but is less emotional. "The country is going to the dogs, and there's not much that either you or I can do about it. The unrighteous element is so strong these days. . . . You can't fight city hall. . . . Nobody will listen anymore to what the Bible has to say."

Others say that while a victory might be won here or there, too many battles are popping up all at once. Sex education, homosexual rights, abortion, pornography, children's rights, women in the military, no-fault divorce—the list runs on, and nobody has energy or time enough to tackle them all. Our only choice is to hunker down in silence and hope the storms don't do too much damage to us personally.

This was the major stance of the Christian church in the first two-thirds of the twentieth century. "This world is not my home; I'm just a-passin' through," the old song went. Many churchgoers didn't see a connection between their faith and a needy world.

Today's apathetic Christians see the connection, at least intellectually, but they quickly go on to state that the odds of improvement really are hopeless. They would like to improve America's moral climate, but realistically they don't see a ghost of a chance, so they elect to save their energy.

3. *Anger.* This response is in stark contrast to the first two. It refuses to give in. With mounting indignation, people declare, "The nation was founded on Christian principles, and we will not surrender to the unbelievers! Stand up for America! Stand up for righteousness! Drive back the forces of wickedness! Fight to the last with every ounce of passion. We've got to, for the sake of our children."

One biblical example is raised repeatedly as a prototype: Jesus driving the merchants out of the temple. He was fired up to attack the moneychangers that day, causing quite a scene as a result. Let's make two observations about that. First, the Son of God's wrath was directed at *religious leaders and workers*—those who made a living from misuse of God's house. He wasn't pitching over tables in the courts of Herod or Pilate. Throughout the Gospels, Jesus did get upset. With whom? Legalistic Pharisees, scribes, priests, rabbis, Sadducees. In other words, the religious power structure got scolded by Jesus while the ordinary sinners were usually welcomed with love.

> *Throughout the Gospels, Jesus did get upset. With whom? ... The religious power structure.*

Second, the image of Jesus getting red in the face is definitely the exception, not the rule. If you take his three years of public ministry as a whole, this was not a Man who specialized in fuming and castigating. He was generally a controlled and even gentle person. Whenever a Hollywood scriptwriter has tried to morph Jesus into an angry revolutionary for the silver screen, the public has generally rejected the film as a distortion.

Nevertheless, anger is a powerful emotion, and in a culture war it pulls people out of lethargy faster than just about anything else. It motivates and energizes. It lends itself to vivid imagery, as in this quotation from a major Christian leader.

> The strategy against the American radical left should be the same as General Douglas MacArthur employed against the Japanese in the Pacific.... Bypass their strongholds, then surround them, isolate them, bombard them, then blast the individuals out of their power bunkers with hand-to-hand combat. The battle for Iwo Jima was not pleasant, but our troops won it. The battle to regain the soul of America won't be pleasant either, but we will win it![9]

This kind of proclamation inevitably raises the hackles of the nonreligious, and a loud argument ensues.

Once the adrenaline is pumping, it is hard to shut it off. The hot lava of anger runs not only at foes, but at friends as well if they fail to help the cause as expected. Especially when fellow Christians seem to hesitate in the moral conflict, they become the target of fierce indignation. Granted, some hesitate because they are afraid, but others may rather be rethinking the issue at hand, evaluating a new angle, questioning whether there isn't a better way to proceed. This can bring down upon their heads a fearsome rebuke.

The ancient wisdom is still true:

> *Refrain from anger and turn from wrath;*
>   *do not fret—it leads only to evil.*
> *For evil men will be cut off,*
>   *but those who hope in the* LORD *will inherit the land.*
>
> *A little while, and the wicked will be no more;*
>   *though you look for them, they will not be found.*
> *But the meek will inherit the land*
>   *and enjoy great peace (Ps. 37:8–11).*

Can it be that, with patient forbearance and trust in God, we might *inherit* the land? The verb is so passive. We don't labor to inherit something; we simply wait for it to come our way in due time. Such a passage stretches credibility. Only the fact that this is God-inspired Scripture forces us to take it seriously.

Hear again the words of William Law from the eighteenth century:

> If I hate or despise any man in the world, I hate that which God cannot hate, and despise that which He loves. . . .
>
> There is no greater sign of your own baptism in the Spirit than when you find yourself all love and compassion towards them that are very weak and sinful, and especially towards those who oppose or misuse you.[10]

4. *Apologetics.* This word, our fourth response to our status as a Christ-Following Minority, has two very different connotations. I use it here in the formal sense of explaining and defending one's beliefs, not in the casual sense of saying you're sorry when you bump someone in a crowded store.

Christians who understand their minority status but still want to influence the culture for good engage in reasonable dialogue about the issues. They control their voice level and even keep a smile on their faces while they present common-sense reasons why A might be a better option than B or C for all concerned. The source of their common sense, of course, is God's wisdom as revealed in the Bible. But Christian apologists don't bring that up, because it would serve only to polarize the listeners into a side debate about whether the Bible is reliable, is allowable in the public square, etc., etc., etc.

I remember watching a news clip of a United States senator—a Democrat, by the way—defending a traditional view by reading to his colleagues from a big, thick King James Version. The words were very true—but not very effective in a political debate among persons of assorted faiths or no faith. One can imagine other senators in the chamber that day rolling their eyes and thinking, *So what?*

Another tack is to push a viewpoint because it's "moral." "The present law on _____ is fundamentally immoral and needs to be changed!" That may be correct. But the statement immediately raises the argument of "immoral according to what authority?" Answer: The Bible—which carries a great deal of clout with many of us and almost none with others. Thus the word *moral* is little more than code language for *biblical* and suffers the same limitations.

What should Christian apologists say instead? We are likely to get further if we speak of policies, laws, and programs that are *effective, useful, helpful, a good example, beneficial in the long run.* These words appeal to people's common sense. This is not compromise or hiding one's light under a bushel. Even the Bible itself does this at times. Moses, the great lawgiver, in telling a new generation of Israelites about the Ten Commandments, encouraged them "to observe the LORD's commands and decrees . . . *for your own good"* (Deut. 10:13, italics added). Isn't that interesting? In addition to God's almighty authority ("Obey because he said so, or else"), there's a practical reason to live God's way: It's good for your health and well-being.

Even if we use such logic, we still may not win the discussion. What we are advocating may be too much for the self-gratifying desires of our fellow citizens. The conversation may finally wind down to a vote of no simply because the majority doesn't want to be inconvenienced.

Sometimes an appeal of "Let's consider what would be good for our children" will win the day, since most Americans like to think of themselves as pro-child—but not if it curbs their own passions and yearnings too tightly.

Christ-followers may expect to lose the discussion half of the time. Ponder this analogy from modern technology: Being a member of the Christ-Following Minority is a little

like being an aficionado of the Macintosh computer! Those
of us who love Macintoshes believe in our hearts that they
are infinitely better and friendlier than IBM compatibles.
The fact that less than one-fifth of the population agrees
with us does not rattle us in the slightest. We go merrily on
our way, enjoying our wonderful machines—and if any IBM
user seems open to seeing the light, we're more than happy
to explain.

So it should be in debates about public policy. More
important than the facts of the matter is the flavor with
which the facts are propounded. The highest truth put forth
in a tone of superiority and judgmentalism is worth little.

As Charles Colson, the one-time White House "hatchet
man" who has mellowed considerably since his conversion
to Christ, writes, "We must defend the truth lovingly, win-
somely, letting others see in all we do the excellence of him
who has called us from darkness into light."[11]

A former president of the National Association of
Evangelicals, after a great deal of experience in this tricky
work of apologetics, said:

> We should not expect those outside the house-
> hold of God to adopt every position firmly rooted in
> Scripture and the Judeo-Christian tradition.
>   By our activism, often poorly conceived and stri-
> dently promoted, we have created an image of rigid,
> prejudiced people. More and more Americans will feel
> entirely justified and respectable saying no to the
> church. They may not be rejecting Jesus, just the people
> who profess to follow Jesus.[12]

The effort to end abortion, to cite just one example, is
often posed in the most military of terms, as a "war." In fact,
the analogy is regularly drawn to the nineteenth-century battle against slavery in the United States: Just as the abolitionists
pressed the fight to free blacks, so Christians today must fight
to protect the unborn. We tend to forget, however, that the

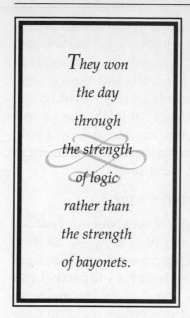

They won the day through the strength of logic rather than the strength of bayonets.

slavery question in America was not settled except by a horrific Civil War that killed 2 percent of the national population and wounded another 1 percent. The goal was right, but the means were ghastly. A comparable toll today would be the deaths of 5 million Americans and the maiming of another 2.5 million.

Perhaps we would do better to take inspiration from the British model. In that nation, William Wilberforce and his friends in Parliament managed to get the slave trade banned without bloodshed. They won the day through the strength of logic rather than the strength of bayonets.

Many moral debates these days center around sexual issues—what is allowable and what is not. This passionate subject arouses passionate rhetoric. Richard J. Mouw makes an excellent observation when he writes: "The whole point of the biblical perspective is to promote a sexuality that is kind and reverent. So it's important that we present the biblical viewpoint kindly and reverently to those with whom we disagree about sexual standards. Not to do so is to undermine our own message. Sexual civility is an important way of living out our commitment to the gospel."[13]

This work of apologetics in an independent-minded society is hard work. It calls for subtlety and nuance. It includes admitting when you have overstated your case and recognizing valid points in the other person's argument. It doesn't deliver the emotional thrill of "winning the battle" against the nasty pagans, like a football game that winds up

34–31 in your favor. We represent a God who doesn't bludgeon sinners into submission. Although he knows best about all things, he woos human beings to come willingly to his point of view. He lays out his truth and then merely opens his arms. Sadly, many people in this world ignore what God is saying; they just "don't get it." For some reason, Almighty God resists the temptation to pick up a bullhorn and repeat the message more loudly. He chooses to stick with his tactics of love and faithfulness.

DOES OUR GOD STILL REIGN?

This brings us to a curious question about our bedrock theology: What does the sovereignty of God—a doctrine Christians all confess—mean in the midst of a culture war?

Every Christian I've ever met believes 100 percent that God *used to be* in charge of this world at the beginning of time: He was the all-wise and all-powerful Creator in Genesis 1. This doctrine is among the first that we teach our children. Similarly, there is widespread agreement that God *will be* in charge of this world at the end. One day he will sit as Judge of every man, woman, boy, and girl. No one will argue with his decisions on that fateful day. Our eternal destiny will rest in his hands.

But what about here and now, in the interim? Is God in charge of the present, or has he momentarily lost his grip? Has America spun off into a renegade orbit that God is unaware of or is powerless to correct?

I don't believe that, and neither do you.

Then why do we act that way?

In thousands of churches every week, Christians stand and sing the popular praise chorus "Our God reigns, our God reigns. . . ." They may even raise their hands, gently swaying back and forth to the words taken straight from Isaiah 52:7. But they go right on worrying and fussing and "stressing" (to use the new verb that epitomizes our time so

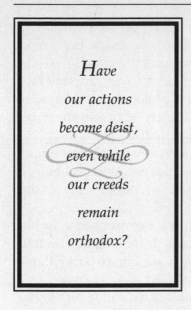

Have our actions become deist, even while our creeds remain orthodox?

well) about what the local school board did the previous week or what the latest tax reform bill failed to include.

I call this the New Evangelical Deism, after the eighteenth-century philosophy that said that God had perhaps created the universe in the beginning but then wound it up like a clock and left it to run on its own. The deists looked around and said, in essence, "There's nobody here to manage things but us. We're in charge for the foreseeable future. God, if there still is a God, is too far away to get involved." Such a perspective is clearly unbiblical.

Have our actions become deist, even while our creeds remain orthodox? It is time for us once again to hear the thunderous voice from Sinai: "The whole earth is mine" (Ex. 19:5). It is time for us to quake at the declaration of Job, whose personal suffering didn't becloud his spiritual perception when he said:

> His wisdom is profound, his power is vast.
>   Who has resisted him and come out unscathed?
> He moves mountains without their knowing it
>   and overturns them in his anger.
> He shakes the earth from its place
>   and makes its pillars tremble....
> If he snatches away, who can stop him?
>   Who can say to him, "What are you doing?"
>
> (Job 9:4–6, 12).

Catch the bemused sarcasm of the Lord in Psalm 50:12: "If I were hungry I would not tell you, for the world is mine, and all that is in it." This is the God preached by Paul to the skeptical crowd at Athens: "The God who made the world and everything in it *is the Lord of heaven and earth*" (Acts 17:24, italics added). Paul had the nerve to declare that fact in the midst of the world center for philosophy and academics, which was teeming with all sorts of pagan theories. "My God is the one in charge," he insisted.

Dozens of other Scriptures say the same thing about this time in the middle of history, after creation and before Judgment Day.[14] God has not lost his sovereign grip on the scepter of the universe. He is still Lord of all.

Granted, God puts up with a lot of nonsense in his domain. He is more passive about evil shenanigans on this planet than you or I would be! We want him to strike flamboyant sinners dead in their tracks. God seems to say, *Don't rush me. I'll get around to dealing with each dictator, each heavy metal rock star, each abortionist, each adulterer in my own time. You'll see.*

As Steven Curtis Chapman sings, "The Lord of the gentle breeze is Lord of the rough and tumble, and he is the King of the jungle."[15]

HOW MUCH HELP DOES A KING NEED?

The foregoing is not meant to imply that the Sovereign Lord of the universe has no employees. He accomplishes some of his goals (although certainly not all—nobody helps him get the sun up in the morning) through "staff." They come in at least two subcategories: heavenly staff, a.k.a. angels, and earthly staff, a.k.a. Christ-followers.

In the current culture war, some very sincere Christ-followers have decided that keeping the public square at least halfway swept and clean is critical to the spread of the gospel. "We have to hold the line against evil in our society," they say, "or the advance of Christianity won't stand a chance." They often use a biochemical analogy, as follows:

"The soil of the culture is growing ever more acidic, what with rampant moral pollution on all fronts. If this is allowed to worsen, the seed of the gospel will be unable to sprout and grow. People will be so wicked they'll be totally impervious to the Good News."

This theory, although well-meaning, does not square with either the Bible or what is actually happening these days around the world. Rather than the gospel being overwhelmed and intimidated by hostile culture, the New Testament teaches a bold principle: "Where sin increased, grace increased all the more" (Rom. 5:20). The gospel is never portrayed as a weak idea needing the help of friendly cultural conditions. It is rather a powerhouse breaking down enemy strongholds. The tougher the opposition, the harder it falls. Consider three modern illustrations.

1. The Christian movement in China had about 1 million adherents in 1949 when Mao Tse-tung and the Communists swept into power. For the next forty-some years, Christians endured the worst conditions imaginable—far worse that we ever have faced in the West. Pastors were hauled off to labor camps, meetings were forbidden, Bibles were unavailable. Today, it is still no picnic to be a Christian in the People's Republic of China. Regular reports tell of opposition and hostility to the faith. Yet the church numbers anywhere from 50 to 80 million believers. Despite the tough, "acidic" environment, new Chinese are coming to Christ at a rate of 30,000 per day.

2. In sub-Saharan Africa (everything south of the Sahara Desert), the growth of the church is estimated to be 20,000 converts per day—this, in spite of struggling economies, drought and subsequent famine, civil war in several places, and stiff competition from Islam to the north. Almost two-thirds of the world's HIV/AIDS cases live in this region.[16] Yet the gospel is making impressive headway.

3. In Latin America, from the Rio Grande to the tip of Cape Horn, the conversion rate is 10,000 a day, again despite the hardships of poverty, governmental corruption, and lack of educational opportunity in many places. All kinds of things need fixing. Prostitution is well entrenched. Drug kingpins scoff at the law. Freedom of worship is sometimes little more than theory. Yet, according to Marcos Witt, a worship leader and evangelist,

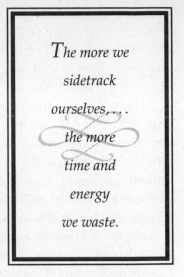

The more we sidetrack ourselves,... the more time and energy we waste.

people are praying in Latin America as never before. All-night prayer vigils are held in homes, churches and public places. These are not just little prayer meetings; they are powerful, loud and insistent rallies, attended many times by hundreds and thousands of people from all over a region....

The Latin Americans are a selfless people, well acquainted with true sacrifice. They are not given to wasting time or resources on superficial and unproductive activity; rather, there is an urgency about them.... [They] know how to make the most with what they have.[17]

Put these three examples together, and we see a gospel surge without the least concern for cultural receptivity. Leith Anderson, Minneapolis pastor and author on the subject of societal change, said, "We read the book of Acts and celebrate the fact that on the Day of Pentecost, three thousand people came to Christ. Today, if you combine mainland China, sub-Saharan Africa, and Latin America, *there's nearly a Pentecost every hour.* Meanwhile, in the United States, we are closing sixty churches a week. The growth rate among white churches in this country is zero—absolutely flat. The only growth we Americans have to talk about is what's happening in the ethnic congregations."[18]

Believers in many other countries have almost no access to the levers of power. They couldn't get a law passed if they tried. They don't even get a tax deduction for the tithes they pay to the Lord. Yet the kingdom of God is advancing powerfully in their lands, to the point that they are now starting to send missionaries to us.

We have much to learn. Our Christian stance in a fallen world is less dependent on external conditions and working majorities than it is on the calling and purpose of the mighty God we serve. Jesus is still in the process of building his church, the gates of hell notwithstanding. He has a blueprint in mind with definite strategies. The more we align ourselves with his plan, the more work that gets done. The more we sidetrack ourselves with doing the job the way we prefer, trying to get non-Christian neighbors and acquaintances to act Christianly without the divine life of Christ inside, the more time and energy we waste.

Five

In Defense of a Little Optimism

Down on the ground level, on the city streets and country roads of North America, what should it be like to live next door to a Christian? How should the neighbors feel about this person who follows Jesus Christ? In the workplace, at the PTA meeting, in the supermarket—what flavor should be noticed?

Some biblical models quickly come to mind.

Daniel in the Babylonian court. Though Daniel took his stand on a dietary issue right at the beginning of his service to King Nebuchadnezzar, making people a little nervous, his overall track record was immensely popular. He "so distinguished himself among the administrators and the satraps by his exceptional qualities that the king planned to set him over the whole kingdom." Even his rivals "could find no corruption in him, because he was trustworthy and neither corrupt nor negligent" (Dan. 6:3–4).

Esther in the Persian court. Although in her heart Esther grieved over the many goings-on in that pagan capital, "the king was attracted to Esther more than to any of the other women, and she won his favor and approval" (Esth. 2:17). Beyond whatever physical charms she may have possessed, she established herself as a respected person in the royal palace for years to come. In due time, Esther politely and diplomatically presented her case for justice and fairness, and a whole ethnic group was protected.

Jesus as a young man. The familiar Luke 2:52 says that in addition to growing tall and wise and godly, Jesus enjoyed "human favor" (NRSV). People in Nazareth just sort of liked him. They didn't think he was strange; they didn't try to avoid him. They smiled when they saw him coming down the street.

The early church in Jerusalem. In spite of the fact that their meetings sometimes got a little noisy, the early believers made a positive impression on their neighbors. Acts 2:47 says that as the days and weeks went by, the believers found themselves "enjoying the favor of all the people." Signs and wonders, such as what happened to Ananias and Sapphira, made for some head-scratching, so that "no one else dared join them, even though they were highly regarded by the people," reports Acts 5:13–14. "Nevertheless, more and more men and women believed in the Lord and were added to their number." This passage definitely shows that the early Christians were *unique;* they didn't just blend in with the majority culture. But at the same time, there was something attractive about them.

New Testament leaders. When the apostle Paul got around to writing down the necessary qualities of an overseer-bishop-pastor (1 Timothy 3), the finale of his list was "He must also have a good reputation with outsiders, so that he will not fall into disgrace and into the devil's trap" (v. 7). Paul was not interested in preachers whom the community saw as weird, harsh, or questionable. He wanted those who could easily connect with the unconverted and be trusted by them.

These examples paint a picture of daily life in a mixed (and mixed-up) society. We don't see a lot of antipathy, resentment, irritation, sloganeering, or showdown. We don't see division into warring camps. Even where there are issues of moral disagreement, the personal link remains respectful and even congenial.

Today amid cultural upheaval, the Christ-Following Minority in my town and yours needs to think about its current reputation. What would it take for non-Christians to begin saying about us, "You know, I don't understand everything about those people, and I don't agree with them on some issues. But they're certainly good to have around. They're a valuable asset to society. I'd hate to see this town, this county, this nation have to get along without them."

A modern illustration comes to mind: the Salvation Army. Probably more than a few people have said, "Their name is terribly antique, and those uniforms aren't my idea of fashion—but they sure do a lot of good for the community. You have to give them credit for making a real contribution."

I'm told that David Yonggi Cho, pastor of the famous Yoido Full Gospel Church in Seoul, Korea—the world's largest, with some 750,000 members—has an interesting rule for his congregation: "No witnessing to your neighbor until after three good deeds." The Christians there are actually *forbidden* to mention the name of Jesus to someone until they have first helped that person fix an appliance, have brought in a meal during sickness, or have shown some

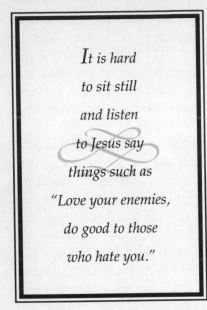

It is hard to sit still and listen to Jesus say things such as "Love your enemies, do good to those who hate you."

other kindness. Cho believes that only after three such acts will the heart be open to the gospel.

WHAT ABOUT ENEMIES?

It is curious to note that the biblical models above all had real-life, fire-breathing enemies. Daniel's foes connived until they finally got him thrown into the lion's den. The wicked Haman almost pulled off a full-scale pogrom against Esther's Jews. The Sanhedrin definitely did not share the opinion on the street about the followers of The Way; that high council managed to put the apostles behind bars more than once and even stoned Stephen to death. Yet the attitude of God's men and women never seemed to sour.

When we face enemies who oppose everything we stand for—hedonists who want to pass out condoms in public schools, for example, or militant activists who want homosexual practice to be a civil right—it is hard to sit still and listen to Jesus say things such as "Love your enemies, do good to those who hate you, bless those who curse you, pray for those who mistreat you. If someone strikes you on one cheek, turn to him the other also" (Luke 6:27–29).

But, Lord ...

"Do to others as you would have them do to you. If you love those who love you, what credit is that to you? Even 'sinners' love those who love them" (Luke 6:31–32).

Well, Lord, I'm not sure you understand Planned Parenthood....

"Be sons of the Most High, because he is kind to the ungrateful and wicked. Be merciful, just as your Father is merciful" (Luke 6:35–36).

At a reception during the Civil War, President Abraham Lincoln made a passing reference to Southerners as "erring human beings"—a much softer term than his audience would have preferred. A woman quickly chastised him for his choice of words. In her mind, they were enemies to be destroyed, and the sooner the better.

> *I caught myself and realized I was seeing society like the Moon, always from one side.*
>
> *—Solzhenitsyn*

"Why, Madam," replied Lincoln, "do I not destroy my enemies when I make them my friends?"

In an odd sort of way, having enemies is good for us. Their opposition makes us think more deeply about what we truly believe, why we believe it, and what our temperament should be during conflict. Aleksandr Solzhenitsyn, the brilliant Russian writer, tells about sharing a room during his years in the gulag with two despicable characters: an air force general who had fallen out of favor, and an MVD (secret police) officer. Both of them represented the suffocating establishment that was squeezing the life out of Russia. Both were miserable oppressors of freedom, not to mention diehard atheists. Both were openly scornful and haughty at having to be around common prisoners.

Solzhenitsyn fumed to himself about their arrogance; he would rather have bunked with almost anyone in the camp than these two men. But in time, he says, his outlook changed. "I . . . caught myself and realized I had always devoted my time and attention to people who fascinated me and were pleasant, who engaged my sympathy, and that as a result I was seeing society like the Moon, always from one side."[1]

The other thing to remember is that enemies can in fact be changed by love. Norma McCorvey, the "Jane Roe" of the infamous 1973 *Roe v. Wade* court decision that legalized abortion, is a case in point. While working at a Dallas abortion clinic, the warmth of an eight-year-old girl, who was the daughter of an opponent, broke through McCorvey's hard shell. She eventually surrendered her life to Christ and speaks today against the killing of the unborn.

Proverbs 25:21–22 says, "If your enemy is hungry, give him food to eat; if he is thirsty, give him water to drink. In doing this, you will heap burning coals on his head, and the LORD will reward you."

The reference to burning coals does not mean what we normally assume—and in fact too often practice these days with verbal flamethrowing. To understand this Scripture, we have to know how homes were heated in the Middle East throughout history. In the center of the room was a low grill with a fire going all the time. Here the family meals were cooked, and family members would gather for warmth whenever the weather turned cold. Every night they would "bank" the fire and hope it lasted until morning while they slept.

If they awakened one chilly morning to a cold room because the fire had gone out, what would they do? (Matches were not invented until 1816.) The most normal recourse was to take a metal pot to a neighbor's home and ask for a few warm coals. If the neighbor was kind enough to help, the borrower would carry the kettle of coals back home in the usual Middle Eastern manner—on the head.

So what Proverbs 25 is describing is helping out your opponent after he or she has done something stupid. Such kindness and generosity to one's enemies are in rare supply these days in our culture war. We are too busy lobbing flaming arrows of rhetoric into the enemy tents. We are seeking to destroy rather than to transform.

Even our choice of terminology tends to polarize. Think for a moment about the common label "pro-family movement." If you are not part of this movement, what does that make you? Anti-family? Few such people intend to hurt families; they simply hold different ideas (some of them unworkable and even counterproductive) about how to help families. But their desire is not nearly as evil as the labels imply.

Many Christians cherish the term *pro-life* and scold the secular press for not using it to describe them. When reporters write "anti-abortion" instead, they are accused of trying to cast a negative light instead of a positive one. The journalists' hesitation may in fact be due to prejudice—but it could also be due to the overreaching nature of the word *pro-life* itself. Where does that leave the opposite side— *anti-life?* With regard to many fetuses, yes, but not across the board.

To understand the subtleties here, consider a different kind of question: How would the proponents of carefully considered, duly decided capital punishment feel about being dubbed "pro-killing"? While there is an element of truth there—the proponent does believe that an intentional mass murderer should be required to give up his own life in return—the label "pro-killing" paints with all too wide a brush. It inflames the debate rather than clarifying it.

These are just two examples of how language can be used to increase enmity. On the other hand, gracious words can go a long way to touch the hearts of those who disagree with us. The Lord can give us all guidance on how to relate to opponents in a way that honors him. The words of Proverbs 16:7 may sound too good to be true, but in fact they are true: "When a man's ways are pleasing to the LORD, he makes even his enemies live at peace with him."

REASON TO LOOK UP

Meanwhile, the world is desperate for good news. Whatever our various disputes, there is widespread concern today about the sagging quality of life. One poll showed 60 percent agreeing with the statement "Children are worse off today than when their parents were kids."[2] Another poll conducted by People for the American Way asked, "Do you think America's best years are behind us, or still ahead of us?" Among males, the vote for "behind us" was 49 percent to 42 percent; among females, the spread was far greater: 58 percent to only 32 percent.

In such a climate, who can find a shred of hope? Who knows where to go for answers? Are there any reasons for optimism? Yes, if you understand that God is still in charge and that his ways still lead to happiness and fulfillment. With Paul we can say, "We are hard pressed on every side, but not crushed; perplexed, but not in despair; persecuted, but not abandoned; struck down, but not destroyed. . . . For we who are alive are always being given over to death for Jesus' sake, so that his life may be revealed in our mortal body" (2 Cor. 4:8–9, 11). Our unique contribution to the world is an outlook that is affirming, confident, and solution-oriented.

Too many of us have taken on the persona of Eeyore in *Winnie-the-Pooh*, the old gray donkey who stood by the side of the stream and looked at himself in the water.

> "Pathetic," he said. "That's what it is. Pathetic."
> He turned and walked slowly down the stream for twenty yards, splashed across it, and walked slowly back on the other side. Then he looked at himself in the water again.

"As I thought," he said. "No better from *this* side. But nobody minds. Nobody cares. Pathetic, that's what it is."

There was a crackling noise in the bracken behind him, and out came Pooh.

"Good morning, Eeyore," said Pooh.

"Good morning, Pooh Bear," said Eeyore gloomily. "If it *is* a good morning," he said. "Which I doubt," said he."

"Why, what's the matter?"

"Nothing, Pooh Bear, nothing. We can't all, and some of us don't. That's all there is to it."[3]

> *Are there any reasons for optimism? Yes, if you understand that God is still in charge.*

We chuckle as adults, but we know the mood all too well. Eeyore has been living in the dumps for so long that he no longer bothers to define just *what* it is that's pathetic. Life is pathetic all around. "We can't all, and some of us don't." No further specifics necessary.

Perhaps we need to go back and read another children's classic from approximately the same period, *Pollyanna*. This young girl is as much a caricature as is Eeyore—but a more useful one. In one scene she tells her friend Nancy why a supper of only bread and milk is fine, just fine. Nancy is incredulous.

"You don't seem ter see any trouble bein' glad about everythin'," retorted Nancy, choking a little over her remembrance of Pollyanna's brave attempts to like the bare little attic room.

Pollyanna laughed softly.

"Well, that's the game, you know, anyway."

"The—*game?*"

"Yes, the 'just being glad' game."

"Whatever in the world are you talkin' about?"

"Why, it's a game. Father told it to me, and it's lovely," rejoined Pollyanna. "We've played it always, ever since I was a little, little girl."

She then goes on to tell the story of her father, a minister, getting a barrel of donated supplies from a church back East. Although he had written that his daughter would like a doll, all that had showed up in the barrel for Pollyanna was a pair of small crutches. Nancy is certain there is nothing to appreciate about this disappointment. But Pollyanna exults, "Why, just be glad because you *don't—need—'em!*"[4]

Well, all silliness aside, which perspective is more helpful in a troubled world—Eeyore's or Pollyanna's? If you have to err in one direction or the other, how about the second rather than the first?

I once saw a poster developed by Mission of Mercy, the outreach that feeds twenty thousand people a day in Calcutta and also runs a hospital, a nursing school, a Bible college, and a large, multilingual church. It showed the city skyline at dusk, the polluted air heavy with smoke from the open cooking fires, the diesel buses, the poorly regulated factories. Across the smoke was printed this quotation from the organization's founder, Canadian missionary Mark Buntain, who passed away in 1989 after three and a half decades of service in that wretched place: "I love Calcutta. I wouldn't want to live anywhere else."

Christians who can find a hopeful perspective on life's problems are infinitely more valuable than people who spend all their time bemoaning, decrying, criticizing, and reproaching. I wonder what you or I would have done had we been in Solomon's seat the day the two prostitutes came in arguing about whose baby was still alive. We would probably have growled about the absurdity of this case, how it would take up valuable court time when the docket was already full. We would have questioned whether either woman could tell the truth on even the smallest detail. We might have launched into an impromptu lecture about how if this pair would get out of their immoral line of work and find honorable employment instead, they wouldn't be bringing children into the world under such pitiful conditions and provoking dilemmas such as this. Next thing they'd probably be applying for welfare and food stamps....

Solomon did none of that. Instead, he looked into the eyes of two human beings and saw the personal tragedy. Beneath the snarling and snapping, he saw two wounded women trying to eke out an existence in an ugly world. He knew their self-respect was nil. He knew they probably hated what they felt they had to do each night but couldn't come up with an alternative. Now they had given birth to wondrous, innocent babies, the only products of beauty for which they could claim credit. And then one had been snatched away in death.

What Solomon saw before his bench was not an abstract social problem requiring government adjudication. He saw two emotional moms pleading for justice. Summoning every ounce of wisdom, he found a way to give them justice.

Do we care about the *feelings* of people or only about *categories* of people? Can we see the human need in the most repulsive individual?

Tony Campolo tells about being invited to speak in Honolulu one time and having trouble getting his body to adjust to the five-hour time shift from his home in Philadelphia.[5] He wound up wide awake at three o'clock in the morning drinking coffee in an all-night diner. Presently the door opened, and in came about eight women laughing and talking loudly. Campolo soon deduced that they were streetwalkers finished with their evening's work and relaxing before going home to sleep. One, named Agnes, mentioned to her friend that the next day would be her thirty-ninth birthday.

After the group left, Campolo got a bright idea. He said to the gruff proprietor behind the counter, "Did you hear that one woman say tomorrow was her birthday? Whaddya say we throw her a party? I'll come back tomorrow night with some decorations, and let's surprise her with a cake and everything!"

The man's wife came out of the kitchen. Both of them said, "That is a wonderful idea. Let's do it."

Twenty-four hours later the little diner was decorated with streamers and balloons. A festive sign was taped to the mirror. The couple had put the word out on the street, and a large assortment of night people were gathered. When the prostitutes came in for their usual coffee, the shout went up: "HAPPY BIRTHDAY, AGNES!"

The woman stood speechless as the singing began. Tears started to roll down her cheeks. Nobody had showed her genuine kindness in years. The owner brought out a birthday cake with candles. Agnes was in such shock that she had to be reminded to blow them out.

She paused again. "Well, cut the cake, Agnes!" the proprietor said.

She finally found words. In a whisper she said, "Please. . . . I just . . . I just want to keep the cake. I'll take it to my apartment down the street . . . just for a couple of days. Please let me keep the cake."

No one knew how to respond, but no one could think of a reason to refuse her request. So out the door she fled, holding the cake as if it were the Holy Grail.

An awkward silence filled the room. Campolo finally broke in with a bold suggestion: "I have another idea—why don't we pray?" Without hesitation he began to voice a prayer for Agnes, that God would bless her on her birthday, that God would bring peace into her life and save her from all that troubled her....

At the amen, the diner owner said, "Hey—you didn't tell me you were a preacher. What kind of church do you preach at?"

Campolo thought a moment, cocked his head sideways, and then answered with a grin, "I preach at the kind of church that throws birthday parties for whores at three-thirty in the morning!"

What happened next was the most poignant moment of all. The man squinted at Campolo and announced: "No ... no, you don't. There is no church like that. *I would join a church like that.*"

All across our world, millions of troubled people are trying to find a way to get through another night, another birthday, another season of life—and assuming the church of Jesus Christ could care less. They think we're mad at them. They think we despise them. They think we think they're no good, and we have a big black Book to prove it.

What they don't know is that the Book actually says, "Let your gentleness be evident to all. The Lord is near" (Phil. 4:5). The compassionate Christ is standing just behind our shoulder listening to every word we say to both friend and foe, watching every act. He waits to see if we have heard his teaching or not.

In another place the Book says, "Love ... is not rude, it is not self-seeking, it is not easily angered, it keeps no record of wrongs. Love ... always protects, always trusts, always hopes, always perseveres" (1 Cor. 13:5–7).

If only that kind of love could infuse our attempts to mold this culture.

Part Two

Friends and Enemies

*RESOLVED, Never to speak evil of any one,
so that it shall tend to his dishonor, more or less,
upon no account except some real good.*

Jonathan Edwards, 1722

Six

Will We See Thomas Jefferson in Heaven?

Wouldn't it be nice if we could go back to an earlier, more wholesome time in America? Wouldn't it be great to live in a country without gangsta rap and sleazy videos, without politicians defending abortion and squelching prayer in school, a place where people went to church on Sunday and lived throughout the week by what they heard there?

That would be wonderful. How about turning the clock back to 1915? Ford Motor Company turned out its millionth car that year; Alexander Graham Bell managed to get a phone call all the way from New York City to San Francisco; Margaret Sanger (founder of Planned Parenthood) was put in jail; and Woodrow Wilson, the home-schooled son of Presbyterian missionaries, lived in the White House and said things like "America was born a Christian nation for the purpose of exemplifying to the nations of the world the principles of righteousness found in the Word of God."[1]

Well, allow me a personal word about the blessings of 1915. In the Indiana heartland, that was the year my Grandmother Flora, a Quaker preacher's daughter only twenty-seven years old, moved with her four young children back to her parents' home to escape the terror of life with an alcoholic husband. James Merrill, whose surname our family bears, had seemed decent enough when they married at Christmastime in 1908, but his drinking had soon gotten totally out of hand. Flora didn't know what to do but flee to safety with her little brood.

By the next February, my grandmother was suddenly dead of jaundice. The children were ages six (my dad), five, four, and twenty-one months. Their father gave no hint of intending to straighten up his life and take responsibility.[2] Flora's parents, like many grandparents today, had little choice but to wipe their tears, take a deep breath, and rise to the need of giving their grandchildren a godly upbringing.

Meanwhile, my mother was growing up in a small Iowa town filled with churches and surrounded by corn-fields. The year 1915 will be remembered as the year her oldest sister, Nora, came back after a disastrous marriage to a man their father could not bring himself to call by name, only "that d—Missourian." Everyone had told Nora that John was up to no good, but she didn't listen. Now she was back, with reddened eyes and slumping shoulders, telling of raucous drinking bouts that had turned into orgies, with John forcing her to be available to any man in the house.

Shattered and humiliated, she spent the rest of her life (fifty years) in a self-imposed penance at home, caring for her aging parents, never imagining herself worthy of a healthy relationship with a man. The family did scrape up enough money for her to go to court and reinstate her maiden name.

"GOOD OLD DAYS"?

That such things could go on in prewar, Farm Belt, small-town America is sobering testimony that this has always been a fallen society. While in those days certain social proprieties prevailed on the surface, the

During the "good old days" they were known as "these trying times."

way people actually behaved revealed their true character. I'm not convinced that my clan was terribly atypical; perhaps you have heard similar stories from an ancestor willing to be honest about the past.

Stephanie Coontz, who teaches at Evergreen State University in Olympia, Washington, writes that in the middle of the nineteenth century, "New York City had one prostitute for every 64 men; the mayor of Savannah estimated his city had one for every 39."[3] Marvin Olasky says that abortion "was as proportionately frequent on the eve of the Civil War as it is now. There were roughly 160,000 abortions in 1860 in a nonslave population of 27 million. (The numbers among slaves are unknown.) This was almost the equivalent of our current figure."[4]

Moving forward to the Depression of the 1930s, Coontz notes that "divorce rates fell, but desertion and domestic violence rose sharply. . . . Murder rates in the '30s were as high as in the 1980s."[5] Come to think of it, even on the old *Waltons* television series about days filled with family warmth and love, the father studiously avoided going to church. Religion was for his wife and children only. Coontz presents her research in a 1992 book entitled *The Way We*

Never Were: American Families and the Nostalgia Trap.[6] Among its shocking revelations are the following.

- While 20 percent of American children live in poverty today, 20 percent of kids in 1900 lived in *orphanages,* often because their parent(s) couldn't afford them. Which is worse—living with a mom and/or a dad without enough money, or living with neither in an institution?
- In the nineteenth century, the age of sexual consent in some states was nine or ten.
- Prior to the 1920s, no law required a divorcing father to pay child support.

After a synopsis of the book appeared in the nation's largest-circulation magazine for seniors, *Modern Maturity,* an elderly subscriber in Philadelphia with a good memory wrote to the editor to say, "During the 'good old days' they were known as 'these trying times.'"

A friend of mine gave me a unique birthday present a few years ago: a mint-condition copy of *Life* magazine from the week I was born, near the end of 1943.[7] On the cover is a black-and-white photo of a U.S. pilot's pretty wife sitting on a window sill eagerly watching for her husband's return. In between ads for Studebaker cars and Philco radios are pictures of Roosevelt and Churchill meeting Stalin at Teheran and of Allied bombs falling on Bremen.

The most intriguing article, however, is entitled "Our Kids Are in Trouble." Says the subhead: "The phenomenal rise in juvenile delinquency during the war is a problem which concerns everyone in the U.S." Photos show teenage boys smoking marijuana and teenage girls waiting on the street to be picked up. "Too many Victory Girls believe it is a part of patriotism to deny nothing to servicemen," one caption reads.[8]

Example after example run on for eight pages in small print, documenting the loose morals and transgressions of young people: a gang rape in the Bronx, a seventeen-year-old in Kansas City who admitted marrying three different girls in less than a year, the Navy having to build a fence around a Detroit armory to keep out the young women. "Train wrecking, hoodlumism, willful destruction of war materials and other property, arson, assault, rape and murder are among the crimes which are on the increase among young boys," the author bemoans.[9] So much for the early virtues of Americans now in their sixties and seventies.

During the same year, Richard Rodgers and Oscar Hammerstein II teamed up to write *Oklahoma*, their first of many smash-hit Broadway musicals. It is still a perennial favorite of high school, college, and community theater groups. Remember the solo by Ado Annie, the silly little flirt who basically knows how to behave on a date: "But when I'm with a feller, I fergit! . . . Soon as I sit on their laps, sump'n inside o' me snaps!" The name of the song: "I Cain't Say No."

And the audience laughs. Here is a musical that completely trivializes romance and marriage, as if choosing a life partner were no more significant than choosing from an ice-cream menu. We go on encouraging today's young thespians to perform these tunes, yet we don't want them to embrace their outlook.

Obviously, America's view of male-female interaction and commitment was in big trouble long before Elvis or the Beatles, let alone today's rock bands. The theory that says America was fine until the rebellious 1960s and then all chaos broke loose simply will not wash. As one Christian writer noted in reviewing the nostalgic book *Our Journey Home* by Gary Bauer of the Family Research Council, "The children . . . produced in the fifties spawned the 'sexual revolution' of the sixties. . . . If the families of the fifties were so conservative, how did the culture change so suddenly?"[10]

I do not point out these things to defame America or its people. In all of the periods mentioned above, there were also godly men and women who raised responsible children and did their best to improve the moral climate of their day. But it is fundamentally dishonest to pretend that their righteousness was the prevailing lifestyle and that the devil was hard up for recruits until Mick Jagger came along.

"INCITEMENTS TO VIRTUE"

Maybe we should go further back—back to the founding fathers. After all, their lofty vision shaped this country in the very beginning. They were men of courage and brilliance. We thrill to their ringing quotes today.

> Whosoever shall introduce into public affairs the principles of primitive Christianity will change the face of the world.
> —Benjamin Franklin

> It is religion and morality alone, which can establish the principles upon which freedom can surely stand.
> —John Adams

> It is impossible to rightly govern the world without God and the Bible.
> —George Washington

> I have always said, and always will say, that the studious perusal of the Sacred Volume will make better citizens, better fathers, and better husbands.
> —Thomas Jefferson

> America is great because she is good, and if America ever ceases to be good, she will cease to be great.
> —French observer Alexis de Tocqueville

In Christian magazines these days, you can even find advertisements for check blanks with quotations such as these etched into the background art.

Unfortunately, four of the above five sound bites (all but the Adams line) are apparently bogus! Eagerness to paint a certain picture has run ahead of scholarship. No less a scholar than David Barton, well-known conservative Christian author and speaker on the Christian roots of America, has published a list of such doubtful quotes—sayings being passed around in the Christian media these days that in fact were never uttered or at least can't be documented.[11]

> *The theory that says America was fine until the rebellious 1960s and then all chaos broke loose simply will not wash.*

The founding fathers did, however, hold a high view of religion, and they welcomed its influence in strengthening the new nation. (They needed it; the populace in 1794 may have been patriotic, but it was also 10 percent alcoholic, according to one estimate.) Anything that would curb the lower nature and get people to treat one another respectfully was a valuable asset. Jefferson spoke approvingly of all "incitements to virtue" that could help elevate society.

Beyond religion, the founding fathers held an even loftier view of the capacity of reasonable men and women to do the reasonable thing. In fact, you will notice them even capitalizing the word *Reason*, as if it were a god of sorts. This shows the influence of the Enlightenment, the secular philosophical movement of the seventeenth and eighteenth centuries that held that human beings are bright enough to solve most problems if they will only apply their minds. Listen to the exuberance of Caesar Rodney, a Delaware lawyer who wrote a letter to Jefferson:

> Every door is now open to the Sons of Genius and Science to inquire after Truth. Hence we may expect the darkening clouds of error will vanish fast before the light of reason; and the period is fast arriving when the Truth will enlighten the whole world.[12]

If only it were that simple....

Perhaps this helps us to understand why the beloved United States Constitution, cherished as one of the most brilliant documents of the ages, does not mention the name of God even once. The fifty-five very intelligent statesmen who gathered in Philadelphia in the summer of 1787 (Jefferson later called them an "assembly of demi-Gods"—a Freudian slip?) felt they had all the wisdom they needed to chart the shape of a government of checks and balances. Only late in the proceedings, when they became deadlocked, did the venerable Benjamin Franklin suggest that maybe they should pause to pray.

When someone questioned Alexander Hamilton about the omission of God's name in the text, he is reported to have simply answered, "We forgot." Washington, ever the smooth diplomat, brushed off the same question by saying, "The path of true piety is so plain as to require but little political direction."

Granted, the Declaration of Independence does refer to God four times. Notice, however, the oblique tone.

First reference: People deserve "the separate and equal station to which the Laws of Nature and of Nature's God entitle them." Shouldn't it be the other way around—"the God who created nature"? If you're a Christian, yes. But not if you're grounded in the Enlightenment, with its high regard for natural law, out of which may (or may not) emerge a notion of the deity.

Second reference: People are "endowed by their Creator with certain unalienable Rights." Jefferson's original draft was hazier; he wrote "that all men are created equal and independent; that *from that equal creation* they ..." (italics added). A committee talked him into being a little more direct.

Third reference: "... appealing to the Supreme Judge of the world for the rectitude of our intentions. . . ." This is a fairly straightforward mention of God as the final evaluator of human conduct.

> *The beloved United States Constitution does not mention the name of God even once.*

Fourth reference: "... with a firm reliance on the Protection of Divine Providence. . . ." There is not much sense of personhood here, just a vague nod in the direction of some benevolent force in the cosmos.

PERSONAL VIEWS

Were the founding fathers perhaps just being coy? Were they trying not to wear their faith on their sleeve so as to avoid needless arguments, but deep down firmly holding God at the center of their worldview, at the center of their personal hope for eternal life?

In some cases, yes. Patrick Henry's faith was undeniably deep. John Jay of New York, first chief justice of the Supreme Court, was equally devout, as was John Witherspoon of New Jersey, the one minister to sign the Declaration of Independence.

Benjamin Franklin, however, liked listening to preachers such as George Whitefield but never got much further than seeing Christ as a good moral teacher. When pressed by Ezra Stiles, president of Yale, on whether Jesus was divine, Franklin diplomatically said that he had never really studied the matter but that he, along with many other deists, had "some doubts."

John Adams, our second president, read the Bible and led a moral life. But when it came to things like the doctrine of original sin, he choked. "I am answerable enough for my own sins," he wrote in 1815. "I know they were my own fault, and that is enough for me to know." His idea of God was "the Power that moves, the Wisdom that directs, and the Benevolence that sanctifies." How's that for vagueness? On the subject of the incarnation and deity of Jesus Christ, he was downright blunt. "This awful blasphemy" needed to be gotten rid of, he wrote in a letter to Thomas Jefferson.[13]

Someone asked James Madison late in life to explain his views on the being and attributes of God. He answered that he had essentially stopped thinking about those subjects fifty years before, while a student at the College of New Jersey (now Princeton). His life had been too occupied with the excitement of the Revolution.[14]

George Washington was more circumspect in his remarks, to the point that it is hard to know where he really stood. When he did speak of God, he usually selected dispassionate terms, such as "the Grand Architect" or even "the Higher Cause." Perhaps we can learn more from his actions. In the decade before his life got hectic during the Revolution, he showed up at his Anglican church only about ten times a year—even though he was a vestryman there. Says one biographer: "His religion, though no doubt perfectly sincere, was a social performance. . . . He seems never to have taken communion."[15]

Once in leadership of the Continental Army, Washington took a laissez-faire attitude toward his soldiers' morals. Church historians tell about a chaplain to Washington's troops, the Reverend Alexander MacWhorter, who inspired everyone on December 7, 1776, with a blistering sermon attacking the "Papist Highland barbarians" (Scottish troops on the other side). "But the irony was that, full of condemnation for British evil as the sermon was, MacWhorter never said one word about the 200 or more camp-following women, perhaps the largest gathering of prostitutes to that day on American soil, who with the troops listened to his sermon."[16]

Finally, what about Thomas Jefferson? He was indeed a brilliant patriot. President John F. Kennedy was probably correct when he said, in a witty after-dinner remark to an East Room full of Nobel prize winners, "This is no doubt the greatest assemblage of genius in this room since Thomas Jefferson dined alone." He more than anyone else was the mind and the pen of our charters of freedom and liberty.

Jefferson read the New Testament daily. Yet, with his Enlightenment loyalties, he could not stomach the "unreasonable" parts. So he actually went to the work of getting his scissors and cutting out the verses that offended him. Out went the miracles of Jesus and the apostles. Out went the Resurrection. Out went all mention of Christ as divine. He pasted together what remained into his own truncated version, forty-six pages "of pure and unsophisticated doctrine," with a title page that read, "The Life and Morals of Jesus of Nazareth, Extracted textually from the Gospels in Greek, Latin, French & English." You can go and see it in a museum today.

No wonder Jefferson stopped proclaiming national days of prayer, fasting, or thanksgiving, as Washington and Adams had done. That was too Christian a thing for a president to do, he concluded. He denounced the idea of the Trinity as "mere abracadabra." The deity of Christ, his resurrection, the divine authority of Scripture—all were the "*deliria* of crazy imaginations." Near the end of his life he admitted, "I am of a sect by myself, as far as I know."

Can such a man, honored though he is, be termed a Christian? Will we see Thomas Jefferson in heaven? Can you actually gain eternal life without placing faith in the atonement of God's only Son on the cross? Not if the Bible's criteria for salvation have any meaning. The chances for Franklin, Adams, and many of the others don't look much better.

RELIGION ON THE SIDE

Now we start to see why the founding fathers gave so little official favor or protection to Christianity. It was a nice religion to have around for its moral influence, but more central in their minds was not to let it run the country. They had had all too much of that back in Europe, with religious wars and partisan excommunications and the rest. They framed a brief amendment that said Congress couldn't "prohibit the free exercise" of religion (so brief a line that we are still arguing in court today, more than two hundred years later, about what the First Amendment really covers and doesn't cover). Beyond that, the churches would just have to make a go of it on their own.

"When a religion is good," wrote Benjamin Franklin, "I conceive that it will support itself; and, when it cannot support itself and . . . [is] obliged to call for the help of the civil power, it is a sign, I apprehend, of its being a bad one."[17]

When Betsy Ross helped George Washington put together the American flag, it marked the first time among Western nations that a Christian symbol—for example, a cross—was *not* included. Just stars and stripes. That was because, in their minds, they were not planting an explicitly Christian nation. They were planting a nation of freedom and opportunity for all.

The most revealing glimpse of how the founding fathers felt about the role of Christianity can be found in a little-remembered 1797 treaty with Tripoli, the capital of modern Libya—a Muslim government. It was negotiated right at the end of Washington's second term, then ratified by the Senate and signed by the incoming president, John Adams. The religious character of America is described in these words: "As the government of the United States of America is not in any sense founded on the Christian Religion,—as it has in itself no character of enmity against the laws, religion or tranquility of Musselmen [i.e., Muslims]

> *To the founding fathers, Christianity was a nice religion to have around for its moral influence, so long as it didn't run the country.*

. . . , it is declared by the parties that no pretext arising from religious opinions shall ever produce an interruption of the harmony existing between the two countries."[18]

Is that not astounding? The official view at the very beginning of our nation was *Please get it straight: You're not dealing with some kind of Christian government here that's going to push its faith down your throat. This is a pure secular agreement we're making, with no hidden agenda.*

Such words almost lead one to ask, did the founding fathers get it right? Were they too afraid of religion in the public square? If they wanted the character-building help of Christianity, shouldn't they have given it more of an official place? Wouldn't we have saved a lot of grief over the last two centuries had they done so?

Maybe so, maybe not. It is too late now to rewrite history. The founding fathers set religion on its own in a free society to make its own mark, win its own converts, and pay its own bills.

THE HOLY COMMONWEALTH

When American Christians today cry for a return to the founding principles, what they have in mind, without realizing it, is less the philosophy of Washington and Jefferson than that of the Pilgrim settlers 150 years earlier. *There* one finds the up-front, openly Christian proclamations:

> In ye name of God Amen. We whose names are underwritten. . .doe by these presents solemnly & mutualy in ye presence of God, and one of another, covenant, & combine ourselves togeather into a civill body politick. . . .
> —The Mayflower Compact, 1620

> We shall find that the God of Israel is among us when he shall make us a praise and glory that men shall say of succeeding plantations: "The Lord make it like that of New England." For we must consider that we shall be a city upon a hill.
> —John Winthrop, on board the *Arbella*, 1630, en route to become the first governor of the Massachusetts Bay Colony

All right now! Here we have a politician with guts. No squirming around with tolerance talk, no fuzziness about eternal truth. This would be the New Israel, a called-out people dedicated to serving Almighty God as earnestly and completely as possible.

Thus it was entirely logical, according to a 1641 Massachusetts law, that "if any man . . . shall have or worship any other god, but the Lord God, he shall be put to death." A person could also get capital punishment for witchcraft, blasphemy, homosexuality, adultery, and kidnapping.[19] On a lesser scale, people also were expected to be diligent in educating their offspring. If they were not, "The selectmen [town councilmen], on finding children ignorant, may take them away from their parents and put them into better hands, at the expense of their parents."[20]

How would you like to put that power in the hands of big government today?

Less than a year after Governor Winthrop arrived, however, a troublemaker named Roger Williams landed. He was a minister, but he didn't buy the idea that this, or any other specific land, could be specially chosen by God. Ever since the coming of Christ, he argued, God had been building a *spiritual* nation of his born-again people, and it wouldn't work to try to set up a temporal "holy commonwealth." The Massachusetts populace dealt with Williams for a few years and finally kicked him out; he headed south to start a new colony called Rhode Island. Cotton Mather, one of the prominent clergy of the day, dismissed him as "the man with a windmill in his head."

Williams was not trying to say that doctrine didn't matter or that moral living was unimportant. On the contrary, he believed the Christian walk was so demanding that no community could possibly be made up entirely of true believers, and therefore it was better not to mix church and state. As the decades went by, other people came around to his view, realizing that the "New Israel" just was not working very well. Immigrants kept coming to these shores for all sorts of motives, commercial and otherwise. How would all the new Americans get along?

In our time, many Christians are decrying the arrival of what they call a "post-Christian culture." Books, speeches, seminars, and broadcasts lament the sad state of affairs. The assumption is that since the election of Bill Clinton, or since *Roe v. Wade*, or since the removal of organized prayer from the public schools, we have slipped into the ditch of a wholly new and dark era in American life.

I agree: Our society is post-Christian. But it has been post-Christian for more than three hundred years. If I had to pick a marker date, it would not be 1992, or 1973, or 1962. It would be 1684, when, after much transatlantic arguing, the

King of England finally revoked the Massachusetts Bay
Colony charter, installed his own governor, and opened up
voting to every landowner (white male, that is), whether
Congregationalist, Anglican, Quaker, Jew, or even infidel.
The Puritan leaders were aghast, knowing full well that this
meant the end of the "Righteous Empire" they had labored
to build and preserve for the preceding sixty-four years.

It was, however, partly their own fault. They had
already given up one of their core values back in 1657 with
the adoption of the "Halfway Covenant," by which people
could join the church (and thus help run the society) without making a personal confession of faith. If people's parents had brought them for baptism as infants and they had
generally behaved themselves since then, that was good
enough.

No wonder daily life in colonial America became
"post-Christian." In 1674, Samuel Torrey wrote: "Truly, the
very heart of New England is changed, and exceedingly cor-
rupted with the sins of the times. There is a spirit of pro-
faneness, a spirit of pride, a spirit of worldliness, a spirit of
sensuality, a spirit of gainsaying and rebellion, a spirit of lib-
ertinism, a spirit of carnality."[21]

By the time Jonathan Edwards came along in the 1730s,
he was an unpopular voice crying in the wilderness against
spiritual coldness. Take as an example his view of the common practice of "bundling." This was a solution for couples
in love who sought a place to talk alone but faced the problem during the New England winters of chilliness in every
room of the house except the one with a fireplace—where
all the other family members were already gathered. It was
generally allowed for the young man and young lady to
retreat to a bedroom and crawl under the quilts (fully
clothed, you understand) for an evening of warm conversation and, uh . . . Edwards criticized this custom as overly
tempting—and was roundly berated by the "good Chris-

tians" of Northampton for having a dirty mind!

Pick any decade you like—you will find undeniable evidence of widespread secularism and disregard for Christian morals. Turn the clock ahead all the way to the 1950s, a time often praised today for its wholesomeness and goodwill. The president during that decade, Dwight D. Eisenhower, revealed the shallowness of

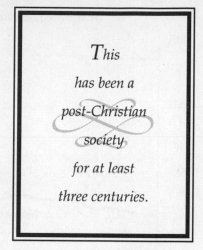

This has been a post-Christian society for at least three centuries.

his Christian understanding when he said, astonishingly, "Our government makes no sense unless it is founded on a deeply felt religious faith—and I don't care what it is."[22]

This is indeed a post-Christian society—no doubt about it. It has been for at least three centuries now. Does this mean we should not respect America? Not at all. I love my country very much. I just do not *expect* a great deal in terms of moral example. To get a picture of true righteousness and moral living, I must look not to the 1920s, or the 1820s, or the 1720s, but to the Word of God.

James Davison Hunter gives a helpful perspective:

> It does not take Aristotle to remind us that *any* social order forged, in whatever part, through democratic processes will be inherently flawed, unstable, and ideologically impure....
>
> The call, then, is for modesty about our political objectives. For one, this means a recognition that America will never really be a city upon a hill, and if it is, it will be by necessity a city whose walls are crumbling and always in need of repair; America will never be a beacon, except one that is not so bright and that is periodically prone to go out.... America will always be flawed. For Christians and many Jews, this is not

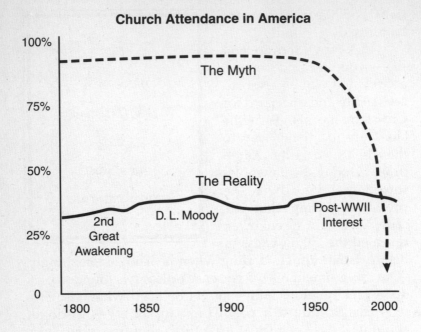

Church Attendance in America

compromise but a frank recognition that the world will always be marred by sin, and that the believer's true citizenship is in heaven.[23]

Os Guinness reinforces this last point when he writes: "For Christians of all people, no part of the past . . . should be considered a golden age—on principle. The Christian's golden age, by definition, is in the future. . . . The pride and gratitude that Christians feel toward the past should be balanced with an acknowledgment of its unfinished work and its darker side."[24]

CHOSEN, OR MERELY BLESSED?

Living today in this land of the free and home of the brave, we may openly say that, despite our shortcomings, we are a *blessed* people. God has given us everything from a temperate climate to rich soil to bountiful mineral resources to usable harbors to stunning scenery. But that is not the same as saying we are his *chosen* people. If we were officially chosen for his special favors, where would that leave the Canadians, the Koreans, the Brazilians, and all the other societies with sizable Christian populations? Would they be second-class by comparison?

We would do well to use the opportunities before us and not waste time pining for "the good old days" of 40 years ago, or 80, or 220, or 370. Church attendance, to return to the yardstick of chapter 4, has not fallen off a cliff; the best available statistics show a more-or-less level line in the 30-to-45 percent zone ever since the early 1800s (see chart). Some liberties to preach the gospel have been curtailed (access to public school students, for example) while at the same time technology has invented new ones (radio, television, videocassette, the Internet) that revivalists Jonathan Edwards and Charles Finney never had the opportunity to use.

Regardless of contemporary problems, hostile attitudes, and trendy relativism, we are not that much worse off than our forebears, and the power of Christ is more than enough to meet the challenge.

Seven

Can Any Good Thing Come Out of Washington?

If you want to trigger a good chuckle these days—whether you're addressing a public audience of hundreds or just talking with friends in a restaurant booth—take a shot at the dummies along the Potomac. It works every time.

We have somehow become a society that despises its government. Cynical bumper stickers and wisecracks abound. "The District of Columbia is forty square miles surrounded by reality" is just one of the more clever lines. It matters not whether you're liberal or conservative, Democrat or Republican. Washington-bashing has become a national pastime.

Not that Washington doesn't deserve the criticism. It has indeed made any number of dubious decisions in recent years. Politicians all too often waste our money, protect their own careers, and abandon common sense. Some of them forget the values they grew up with—or even the values they preached from the stump during their most recent election campaign. Instead of striving for solutions, they make problems worse.

And when they do, we let them know—vociferously. That is part of the American way, we believe. It's like yelling at the umpire of a baseball game. We reason, *I paid my ticket, and now I get the privilege of hollering about anything I don't like. That's how the tradition works.* Without this hue and cry, our newspapers would have a hard time filling up the front page each day. So-and-So said this or that about the president or Congress or the Supreme Court, which evoked a response from someone else, and so on.

In the years since the election of a Democratic president in 1992, the objections from Christian opponents have shot upward. "A vote for Bill Clinton is a sin against God," declared Operation Rescue leader Randall Terry back in the beginning. Christian magazines are willing to take advertisements for sarcastic bumper stickers that read, "I Won't Vote for Rodham and Gore-morrah."[1] Other attacks are not quite as snippy but still carry a punch. I point this out not to defend Mr. Clinton—I personally have never voted for him—but to illustrate the current displeasure.

So many critical letters have been sent out to hundreds of address lists that our language has a new term for it: *fright mail.* The essence is, *Your rights or beliefs are getting hammered by the Washington administration—so send us money now.*

Even when Washington occasionally leans in the direction of doing the right thing (wonder of wonders!), the conservative Christian community is sure there must be a trick somewhere. A 1996 example was the Defense of Marriage Act, a bill to clarify that marriage is "only a legal union between one man and one woman." This concept (which is quite biblical) was put forward in response to the state of Hawaii considering a wider definition that would accommodate homosexual couples.

President Clinton said he agreed with the bill and would sign it once it reached his desk. What did his opponents think of that? They couldn't believe their ears. One popular Christian magazine said, "Clinton's position seemed less a matter of personal conviction than one of political expediency."[2] How so? No specifics were offered, no proof of guile.

Another prominent Christian spokesman declared, "I must admit that I'm suspicious that his statement today is merely part of the now well-publicized effort to look like a conservative candidate for president."[3]

In other words, the man from Arkansas could do no right. Surely he wasn't serious. When, after the bill passed both the House and the Senate, he did in fact sign it into law just as he had promised, his Christian detractors could not bring themselves to give him credit just this once. He must have had some ulterior motive.

Such is the acrid climate of political life in America.

BIRDS OF FRAY

For Christ-followers, how does this square with the teaching of Scriptures such as Ecclesiastes 10:20?

> *Do not revile the king even in your thoughts,*
>   *or curse the rich in your bedroom,*
> *because a bird of the air may carry your words,*
>   *and a bird on the wing may report what you say.*

Far from worrying about being quoted, today's critics want the (satellite) birds of the air to beam their words far and wide.

How do we get around Paul's words to the church in Rome—the Washington of its day? "The authorities that exist have been established by God.... Therefore, it is necessary to submit to the authorities, not only because of possible punishment *but also because of conscience....* Give everyone what you owe him: If you owe ... respect, then respect; if honor, then honor" (Rom. 13:1, 5, 7, italics added). This is not an obscure passage. It makes its point very clearly. We have no plausible case to seek an exemption from obeying. It won't work to argue, "Well, we're in a special situation today." Our government is no more vile than the one Paul was writing about, a point we explored in chapter 3. We are stuck with Romans 13 whether we like it or not.

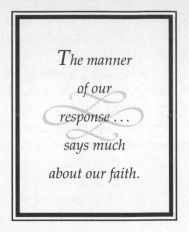

The manner of our response ... says much about our faith.

Neither is it credible to say that we fulfill our duty to this passage by not engaging in open rebellion against the government—that is, civil disobedience—while continuing a verbal barrage. Such assault may be legal in America, but it misses the Christian point of "respect" and "honor" (Rom. 13:7). Paul teaches that there is a matter of conscience here (v. 5). The manner of our response to those with whom we disagree says much about our faith. If we spin the facts to make a politician look murky, if we are careless with his or her reputation, if we are uncharitable in our tone, we have not represented our Lord well.

Dr. Josef Tson, who as a Romanian pastor was persecuted during the Communist era until his exile to the United States in 1981, tells about being confronted with this Scripture by a colonel, one of six on a secret-police tribunal that could sentence him to up to fifteen years in prison. The man taunted Tson with the biblical mandate to cooperate with the authorities.

"Sir," I interrupted, "would you let me explain how I see Romans 13 in this situation?"

He smiled ever so slightly; maybe he was curious. "All right, go on."

"What is taking place here is not an encounter between you and me," I began. "This is an encounter between my God and me."

His expression grew puzzled.

"My God is teaching me a lesson. I do not know what it is. Maybe he wants to teach me several lessons. I only know, sir, that you will do to me only what he wants you to do—and you will not go one inch further—because you are simply an instrument of my God."

He did not like that interpretation of Romans 13, but I did! To see those six pompous men as my Father's puppets! They immediately consigned me to six months of interrogation, five days a week, sometimes up to 10 hours a day.

But in the end, I was right: I learned a great deal.[4]

Should we not be humbled by such a perspective? Here is a Christian who understood that this was still his Father's world regardless of the state's wickedness. He held the "view from the sky" to which we alluded in chapter 1. Whether dealing with a good government, a mediocre government, or an outrageous government, it doesn't change the fact that Christ-followers, always protected by a Higher Authority, are called to behave in a certain way.

Josef Tson goes on to tell how this actually worked out in his life. An awful Monday afternoon came, some four years later, when in the midst of being interrogated by two officers,

a general came into the room. He signaled with his hand for them to leave.

He began to curse me and hit me, slapping my face and hitting my head with his fist, finally knocking my head against the wall.

I screamed—intentionally. I shouted so the other detainees in nearby rooms would hear me. What the general was doing was clearly illegal....

He kept on for a while, then left without another word. The two officers came back and resumed the interrogation as if nothing had happened.

On Thursday afternoon, the general returned. Again he motioned with his hand for the two to leave. I braced myself for a second round of beating.

But the man sat down behind the desk and said, "Don't worry. This time I am calm. I have to come to talk to you."

Now the Lord has promised that when his people are questioned, the Holy Spirit within them will do the talking. I can testify to this truth. I myself was surprised as I said, "Mr. General, because you came to talk to me, I want first of all to apologize for what happened Monday."

He was very surprised.

"Let me explain what I mean," I said. "On Tuesday ... I had plenty of time to think. All of a sudden, it dawned on me that this is Holy Week.

"Well, sir, for a Christian, nothing is more beautiful than to suffer during the time his Saviour and Lord suffered. When you beat me, you did me a great honor. I am sorry for shouting at you. I should have thanked you for the most beautiful gift you could ever have given me. Since Tuesday I have been praying for you and your family."

I saw the man choking. He tried hard to swallow. Then, somehow, he said, "Well, I shouldn't have done it. I am sorry—let's talk."

We talked many days after that. Eventually he said, "Would you put on paper all you have said to me? I want the president of the country to read it."

From this I learned that no one—not even a Communist—is beyond the reach of Calvary love. These are savable people, redeemable people like anyone else. They desperately needed to see Christ in me.[5]

For those of us in the Western world, with all its marvelous guarantees of religious freedom, here is a powerful lesson. We too are dealing with "savable people, redeemable people." Does our manner draw the elite of Washington toward the gentle Savior? Is there the slightest chance that Jesus' love might break through their hardened façades because of what they experience in contact with us?

HOW TO WRECK A DEMOCRACY

This discussion of attitude and conduct is important for a secondary reason—namely, that our political system is more fragile than a Communist state. While dictators may force compliance and order by raw power, we in a democracy have to talk to each other. We have to come to consensus. We have to reason with each other. No wonder George Washington (deist or not!) sent out a prayer to all the state governors on June 8, 1783, which read, in part:

Almighty God, we make our earnest prayer that Thou ... wilt incline the hearts of the citizens to cultivate a spirit of subordination and obedience to government, and entertain a brotherly affection and love for one another....

And finally that Thou wilt ... dispose us all to ... demean ourselves with that charity, humility, and pacific [i.e., calm] temper of mind which were the characteristics of the Divine Author of our blessed religion, and without an humble imitation of whose example in these things, we can never hope to be a happy nation.

What I hear in this prayer is: *Dear God, please help people to calm down and give government the benefit of the doubt—or else this new country simply isn't going to work.* Washington

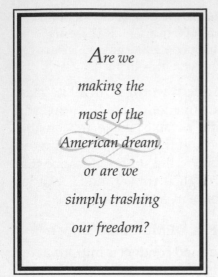

Are we making the most of the American dream, or are we simply trashing our freedom?

knew instinctively that resistance and irritation and mistrust had the power to wreck the whole American experiment.

In the face of today's flak, a record number of United States senators—fifteen out of the thirty-four up for reelection in 1996—decided not to run again, even though most of them easily could have won. More than half were still in their prime years. Why did they quit?

"Politics is broken," said Senator Bill Bradley, a moderate New Jersey Democrat and a former Rhodes scholar widely appreciated on both sides of the political aisle. "People have lost faith in the political process.... Being part of government in a time of distrust is like walking across terrain camouflaged with pits with sharpened poles at the bottom."[6]

Another departing senator, William Cohen, a Republican from Maine, added, "Those who serve are no longer held in respect.... Because of the never-ending flow of negative news, suddenly every trip is [viewed as] a junket, when in fact, many trips we take benefit the American people and American business."[7]

If your mind-set is that nothing good comes out of Washington, you may read such comments with glee. *Send the bums home to earn an honest living for a change.* My response is rather one of sadness. When intelligent, thoughtful men and women with enough initiative to run for public office and serve their country end up ravaged and disheartened by citizen abuse, are we not all losers? Is this really the way democracy is supposed to work? Are we making the most of the American dream, or are we simply trashing our freedom?

Bruce Barron, a Christian who formerly served as an aide to Congressman (now Senator) Rick Santorum, a Pennsylvania Republican, writes, "The most important political battle facing us today may not be between Left and Right, but over whether we will be able to maintain the terms of engagement without which we can no longer have a productive debate at all. Christians should be ideally suited to serve not just as combatants in the culture wars but as bridgebuilders."[8]

> *Not all is as it should be in the District of Columbia, but neither should the place be torched.*

In an insightful editorial entitled "Beware the Adversary Culture," Mortimer B. Zuckerman, editor-in-chief of *U.S. News & World Report,* wrote: "In . . . a vindictive culture it is virtually impossible to rally the nation or to bind its wounds. We are living in a time. . .that strains the connective tissues of many individuals to marriage, family, school, church, nation, job—indeed, to any sense of responsibility." This was written shortly after the Oklahoma City bombing, which explains the context of the following:

> Even more worrisome than the crazies is the depth of anger and alienation felt by ordinary people for government, our politicians and our bureaucrats. . . . Irritation with bureaucrats and excessive taxes is widespread—and understandable—and merits our concern, but blanket denunciations of government are pointless and counterproductive. Government will have to play a role in evolving new ways of coping with the vast changes we face; and it can only do it

while we recognize that democracy depends on talk
and compromise, goals and values.[9]

A friend of mine has learned the slow way about that
needful role of government. More than twenty-five years
ago, he and his wife began a ministry to troubled teen girls,
setting up a residential program complete with a Christian
school and intense discipleship training. Since then, many
young ladies have turned their lives completely around
with the help of this dedicated couple.

In the early years, my friend got into a serious battle
with state officials over various regulations they wanted to
apply. His facilities would need certain equipment, he'd
have to secure various permits, and so on. He considered
this an encroachment of government upon the free exercise
of religion and said so passionately. The face-off even made
the local newspapers.

In time he came to realize that what the state was
requiring was not inherently unreasonable. The bureaucrats
were simply trying to make sure the girls were in a safe and
healthy environment. Compliance with the regulations was
not surrendering to anything sinister; it was merely common sense.

In fact, my friend has even seen times when government proved to be his ally in the ministry. He wrote me
recently about being called to a large city "where a district
attorney was wanting to send a girl to our facility, and I was
asked to attend the hearing. Parents had actually tied this
girl to a chair in their home and had very definitely abused
her. But, there they were with their Bibles in the courtroom,
trying to make everybody think they were right in what
they had done." In such instances, the use of government's
power is entirely appropriate. If we have in the past mainly
engaged in scorning, criticizing, questioning, and accusing
the government, it will not be effective when we need it.

Is it not dangerous, in fact, to teach our children that Washington is a mess, judges are crooked, politicians are all liars, and even the police are dim-witted? Do we really want to go down that road? It leads to anarchy. Without duly constituted authority, imperfect though it may be, we will find ourselves with worse lawlessness than we have now.

No one is saying that the president or the governor is above questioning. These people are members of the fallen society just like the rest. Their errors should not be papered over. But that is not the same as calling them idiots and fools.

If we have gotten to the place where a walk through the marble halls of Congress or a stroll down the Mall toward the Washington Monument raises feelings of disgust and resentment rather than feelings of patriotism and appreciation, we have lost something very precious indeed. Not all is as it should be in the District of Columbia, but neither should the place be torched.

A CHANGE OF HEART

On an even more pragmatic note, what does it take to be effective in influencing the federal government? How does one bring about an improvement in moral perspective?

Another friend of mine, formerly a pastor and college president, moved to the Washington, D.C., area a few years ago to give himself to quiet ministry among government leaders. In the early mornings you can find him (if you know where to look!) leading Bible studies with small circles of U.S. representatives, department heads, or foreign ambassadors. Throughout the day he meets one on one with powerful senators and judges who have requested spiritual guidance.

I asked him once what people such as these say when skewered by phone calls, mail, and faxes from Christian critics. He answered with a story about one congressman, a Democrat from the Midwest, who had been solidly pro-abortion until he came to know Christ personally through a small group around 1980. Thereafter, his views changed.

"He told me one day," my friend reported, "that he hadn't switched sides because people confronted him or carried placards past his office window. 'You have to remember that guys like me didn't get to Washington by being wimps!' he said. 'We're tough. You push me, and I'll push you right back. So what happened to me? I started reading about Jesus. I saw his respect for life—and he changed my heart.'"

> *It is not the call of the church to legislate righteousness, but to demonstrate it.*
>
> *—Paul Cain*

Christian activists who think Washington politicians with certain views can be pressured into adopting opposite views if the voter heat gets high enough, fail to understand human nature. Even seeming victories can turn out to be temporary if they go against the politician's true convictions.

Federal and state governments are capable of doing good. Who of us is not grateful for hydroelectric projects that bring cheap electricity to our homes, or for a military complex that defends our safety? It is not fair to say that politicians are nothing but leeches. We need their service.

At the same time, let us be honest enough to admit that many problems are for *us* to resolve, not them. Paul Cain, a contemporary minister with a prophetic gift, believes God impressed him with some definite insights immediately after the election of 1992. He wrote these in a newsletter published soon afterward. While some readers may be skeptical about people receiving prophetic "words" in our time, let these excerpts from Cain's message stand or fall on their own merits:

- The reason for much of the degeneration of morals in America is not the government's fault, but the church's—for complaining instead of praying, fearing instead of believing. When the church stops complaining about the government and starts repenting of her own sin, the Lord will begin to move in spite of the most resistant government leaders.

- Many who may appear to be on the right side of the moral issues have . . . a combination of unrighteous judgment, spiritual pride and a spirit of control that will not tolerate differences in others.

- Some respected Christian leaders will actually start to rejoice that they now have a perceived enemy in the White House—because of the amount of money they can raise in their crusade to fight him.

- It is right that we should hate sin, but the spirit of intolerance that has gained influence in the church and in some of the right-wing political movements has pushed them across the line into extremism, causing them to sow hatred and division between people.

- Some, in taking a stand against abortion and other injustices, have allowed hatred to enter their hearts. . . . Lives are lost because of abortion, but souls are lost because of this hatred.

- We must not continue to worship at the feet of political movements, trying to get the government to do the church's job. . . . It is not the call of the church to legislate righteousness, but to demonstrate it, and to preach it from the platform that God has ordained.[10]

Washington, in the eternal perspective, is only one governmental center in one nation on one continent of this one planet in one corner of God's great universe. God cares about what goes on there, but he is not in the least stymied by its machinations. His far greater purpose in the world will be carried out by people who understand Who is truly in charge.

Eight

The Clumsiness of Laws

Suppose we wanted to pass a law against impatience. It is, to be sure, one of the worst behaviors of life. In proposing such a law, we would not face much opposition from the public. There would be no "pro-impatience" lobby. Nearly everyone, whether religious or not, agrees that forbearance is a virtue, and impetuous, insistent, gotta-have-what-I-want-right-now people make the world a nastier place.

We wouldn't have to bolster our campaign with Bible verses such as Proverbs 12:16 ("A fool shows his annoyance at once, but a prudent man overlooks an insult") or Ephesians 4:2 ("Be completely humble and gentle; be patient, bearing with one another in love"). Everyone who as a child heard Aesop's fable about waiting for the goose to lay its golden eggs, or was inspired by the story of Thomas Edison trying to perfect the light bulb, would already be on board. The benefits of requiring Americans to be more patient are obvious.

Let's see, now—how should this law be worded? We would have to spell out exactly what constitutes an infraction, of course. Honking one's horn should be prohibited unless the driver in front of you has ignored the green light for at least seven seconds. Honking the horn to get one's spouse or teenager out of the house and into the car would be prohibited under all circumstances. Complaints to a restaurant maitre d' about slow seating should be permitted only in accordance with a mathematical formula based on total occupancy of the building divided by the number of customers waiting, moderated by the number of servers available to work that particular evening divided by the square root of the number of dishwashers in the back. . . .

Penalties should be set according to a scale of fines, starting at fifty dollars and ranging upward to five hundred, depending on the flagrancy of the infraction—for example, whether the victim of the impatient outburst was a family member, a female, or a minority; whether the accused was a repeat offender; whether the expression of impatience was further intensified by rude language or gestures. . . .

Do you see where this is leading?

Some things are very hard to regulate by force of law, although the attorneys of the world delight in trying. "There oughta be a law . . ." goes the popular saying—but in many cases, there isn't. Why? Because written statutes are too often clumsy at getting to the heart of what a society should and should not do.

Think for a moment about the Ten Commandments. How many of them are backed up with legal ordinances in America today? I can identify only three:

- Thou shalt not murder.
- Thou shalt not steal.
- Thou shalt not give false testimony [in court] against thy neighbor.

We used to have laws about honoring Sunday, but those have pretty much faded away. Some states (North Carolina, for example, among others) still have laws against adultery, but they haven't been enforced in generations. The Puritans had laws against misusing God's name, but those are long gone. The rest of the Ten Commandments are almost patently impossible to legislate. How would you write a law against coveting, for example? How would you forbid the dishonoring of father and mother in any enforceable way?

Some other things that are clearly wrong according to the Bible but are hard to ban by legislation are

- Greed
- Rage
- Ignoring the poor, the fatherless, the foreigner
- Religions that don't exclusively honor the one true God
- Lust
- Gluttony
- Divorce
- Racial prejudice
- Witchcraft
- Premarital and extramarital sex between consenting adults
- Intoxication (there are laws against public drunkenness, but not for private situations)

The most brilliant legislative minds simply cannot think up enough laws to make all 265 million of us behave ourselves all the time. Laws are intrinsically ham-handed, failing to get to the motives of the heart. Confucius said long

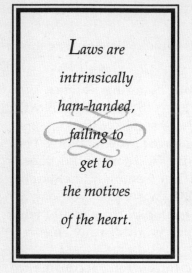

Laws are intrinsically ham-handed, failing to get to the motives of the heart.

ago, "No amount of legislation can take the place of the natural social order provided by the family."[1] And to that, Christians would add "or provided by God's moral code."

Even in matters not usually considered religious, the law fumbles and stumbles. An example comes from Thomas Sowell, articulate thinker and author who belongs to an ethnic group terribly abused in the past (African Americans) and thus the intended beneficiaries of make-good legislation.

You have entrepreneurs coming over here, let's say from India, to set up businesses in the Silicon Valley and being instantly entitled to affirmative action, which has been justified to the public on the grounds that this is redress for past injustices. Such bizarre situations—and they are by no means rare in the United States today—show what a blunt instrument the law is. Once you've put the words on paper, regardless of what you may have originally meant, they take on a life of their own, and you're stuck with the results.[2]

THE BIBLE TOLD US SO

If anyone should fully understand the weaknesses of the law, it should be New Testament Christians. We have a big Book that educates us in great detail, with multiple illustrations, about "what the law could not do, in that it was weak" (Rom. 8:3 KJV). In this case, the apostle Paul was referring even to laws written with the finger of God himself, who is infinitely smarter than all the elected legislators of the country combined.

A major point of the epistles to the Romans and to the Galatians, among others, is this: *Writing down rules and regulations in the hope of containing human behavior is a wearisome and, in the end, futile exercise.* The entire Old Testament bears witness. Activist Christian movements today that say they are "standing for righteousness" would do well to review Galatians 3:21–22: "If a law had been given that could impart life, then righteousness would certainly have come by the

> *We have contented ourselves with advocating "band-aid remedies" for the symptoms of social decay.*
> —Paul Weyrich

law. But the Scripture declares that the whole world is a prisoner of sin." The truly effective cure for societal wickedness is not more federal mandates but rather the life-changing, addiction-breaking, heart-cleansing work of Jesus Christ through the Holy Spirit.

Then why do we think we can clean up people's deeds by external edicts? In the search for good behavior, why do we keep taping oranges onto dead telephone poles and then wonder why they don't grow? The pole may be roughly the same shape as a live tree trunk, but if there's no protoplasm moving through the internal xylem and phloem, no fruit will be forthcoming.

Says Charles Colson, the one-time Washington lawyer who now heads up Prison Fellowship, "That's one of the weaknesses of the Evangelical movement today—that it is so obsessed with politics. It believes that there's got to be a political solution to everything."[3] Granted, the public law is something of a teacher, and it can make things uncomfortable for those who transgress. But the law's weakness is painfully evident to anyone who has looked at a court docket recently. Neither fines nor jail terms are accomplishing a great deal in curbing the appetites of the Independent Majority.

I appreciate the honesty of Paul Weyrich, fund-raiser par excellence for the religious right and the man who first coined the phrase "moral majority" in a meeting with Jerry Falwell. In his book *Taking Stock*, he admits:

> As cultural conservatives, we have a trivial agenda.... What I mean is that, if all the policies we have called for were put into effect tomorrow, the basic trends in our culture, the trends that are bringing about our decline as a nation and as a civilization, would not be changed. They would be slowed but not reversed.... We would not bring about the spectrum shift we need.
>
> We have contented ourselves with advocating "band-aid remedies" for the symptoms of social decay, which is somewhat like taking aspirin for appendicitis.[4]

What a sobering but accurate admission from a man who has generated millions to advance the contemporary conservative agenda.

THE LAW: A MODEST HELPER

Then why bother with laws?

Laws serve a practical purpose in informing the public of what is tolerable in this society and what is not. The young teenager, the newly arrived immigrant, and even we well-entrenched old-timers are thereby notified that in the United States it has been decided by consensus that, for example, we will not drive our cars on the left side of the road. We won't force other people to go places they don't want to go (kidnapping). We will tell the truth on our income tax returns. We will not discriminate on the basis of someone's race, color, religion, or gender. And so forth.

In building such a list, we have not even come close to covering all the bases. We've hardly been able to reach agreement on these few! If you or I were named Dictator-for-Life and given unlimited power, we could whip out a whole new set of laws in short order that would plug a lot of holes. But that's not the way America operates.

Many Christians will argue passionately that laws must have a moral base. They must arise, it is said, out of a foundational Judeo-Christian ethic. The congressional bills and court decisions have to be erected upon an enduring code of righteousness.

To that, I reply, *No, they don't.* I wish they did. I wish every law in this country were required to trace back to God's unerring law. But that's not the way the game is played in the United States. Article I, Section 7, of the Constitution does *not* say, "Every Bill which shall have passed the House of Representatives and the Senate, shall, before it becomes a Law, *be reviewed to ensure its harmony with the Judeo-Christian ethic* and then be presented to the President. . . ." Like it or not, we live under a system in which a law is nothing more substantive than what 51 percent of our elected representatives will vote for, the president will sign, and the Supreme Court will leave alone. That's all. It's a terribly human-based arrangement. Moral foundations are not guaranteed. And the American populace is "congenitally moderate," to use Charles Krauthammer's phrase;[5] it instinctively goes for the middle of the road. If truth happens to be at one edge, voters would prefer to "split the difference."

This society respects laws only when they are developed by group process. Even then, not everyone agrees, and some may go out to flaunt the law and take the consequences. The classic example in our history was Prohibition. In 1919 a majority of the country said, "That's it—no more alcohol. We've had enough devastation and heartbreak over the decades. Throw it out." The only trouble was, too many

Americans said to themselves, "Oh, yeah? Just try to stop me. I don't care if the Eighteenth Amendment is the law of the land. I'll make the stuff in my bathtub if I have to." And after major cultural disruption and disobedience to the law, a surge in organized crime, and deaths due to lethal brews, we finally reached the weary point in 1933 when we said, "All right, forget it. This isn't working. We don't have enough 'consent of the governed' on this issue. Go ahead and drink if you want to." Since that day, millions of Americans, myself included, have continued to believe that alcohol is nothing but trouble and have taught our children the same. We've made a personal decision to abstain whether the law agrees with us or not.

It might be worth asking whether the abortion battle is not in many ways a similar issue to Prohibition. After all, alcohol kills too—an estimated 100,000 people annually, and that number would be far worse were it not for the 1.7 million DUI arrests each year. If the police gave alcohol a free rein the way they do abortion, who knows how many funerals would result?

The pro-life community earnestly believes that abortion is a subcategory of murder and ought to be banned in the same legal way that murder is. Hence the call for a Human Life Amendment to the Constitution—the same approach used with liquor. That would be fine *if* the American people would give general respect to the law once it was passed. Would they? Or would many people insist on killing their unborn even if they had to risk paying a fine or going to jail?

I suspect the latter.

Steven T. McFarland, director of the Center for Law and Religious Freedom, makes a forthright admission when he says, "The fate of the unborn is ultimately sealed not in courtrooms, legislative chambers, or on sidewalks, but in the heart and mind of each woman with an unwanted pregnancy. We

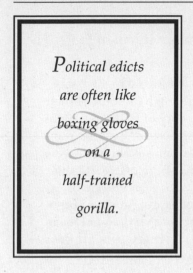

Political edicts are often like boxing gloves on a half-trained gorilla.

must focus on persuading the pregnant woman, rather than a judge or politician."[6]

Stephen Carter, professor of law at Yale University and a committed Christian, adds this interesting observation:

My concern about *Roe v. Wade* is that it changed what was a vibrant and thoughtful moral, cultural, and political debate into a legal debate. We do that all too often, and it's unfortunate. It allows one side to say, "I don't have to listen to you because I have a constitutional right." While that's sort of technically true, you can't really have a discussion in that atmosphere. . . .

It's not that abortion is an unimportant issue. The problem is we're talking about it in a political era in which we seem unable to conduct productive public discussion of important issues. We talk about abortion, but we don't talk about it, really. We yell. We scream. We sneer.[7]

Lest I seem totally discouraging, let me point out a different issue on which we have been able to build more consensus: the control of obscenity. It's actually quite amazing, when you stop to think about it, that legislatures populated by members of various religious persuasions, or none at all—and comprised mostly of males—have been willing to vote against sexy pictures. This has indeed proven to be, as Dr. James Dobson has termed it, "a winnable war." Winnable in part, at least. The hard-core pornographers are not totally out of business, but they are seriously curtailed, thanks to society's consensus against their demeaning products.

Maybe this is a good case study for examining the usefulness of laws. Richard J. Mouw, president of Fuller Theological Seminary, leads the way.

> What about legislation that would make it more difficult for people to follow through on some of their sinful sexual impulses? I am wary of efforts to establish laws whose primary purpose is to force non-Christians to conform to Christian sexual norms. . . . The Scriptures call human beings to offer God their free obedience. . . .
>
> In a pluralistic society, people can produce pornographic movies and literature. But that does not mean they are free to run explicit advertisements for their wares on the pages of the daily newspaper. Nor should our children be confronted with racks of sexually explicit books and magazines when they buy their candy bars at the convenience store down the street. We have no automatic right to keep other people from sinning—but neither are we obligated to make it *easy* for them to pursue their warped designs.[8]

A PLAN OF ACTION

In the final analysis, the Christ-Following Minority must do several things:

- Clearly understand from Scripture what God considers to be right, just, and holy. Make sure to consider *all* God's concerns, not just the ones being talked about in Christian media this month.
- On the personal level, follow God's path to the fullest extent, no matter how inconvenient or unpopular.
- "Always be prepared to give an answer to everyone who asks you to give the reason for the hope that you have. But do this with gentleness and respect" (1 Peter 3:15–16).

- As a citizen, help build what consensus you can in the society for morality.
- Don't expect too much from laws. As James Davison Hunter notes, "Politics, in the final analysis, is primarily effective in dealing with administrative tasks. It is not able to deal with the collective search for shared meanings, the formation of public philosophies of public good, or the organic generation of civic obligations, responsibilities and trust among the citizens who inhabit a community or society."[9]

Political edicts are often like boxing gloves on a half-trained gorilla. The animal tries to aim accurately, but he ends up hitting a lot of unintended targets and causing a lot of trouble. In contrast, "the word of God is living and active. Sharper than any double-edged sword, it penetrates even to dividing soul and spirit, joints and marrow; it judges the thoughts and attitudes of the heart. . . . Everything is uncovered and laid bare before the eyes of him to whom we must give account" (Heb. 4:12–13). In pursuing God's purpose in a modern world, his supernatural sword is considerably more effective than our homemade boxing gloves.

Nine

The Noxious,
Necessary
News Media

If Christians find themselves unhappy with politicians
explored in chapter 7) and lawyers (chapter 8), the
even more exasperated with today's journalists. N
every morning newspaper and every evening news
seems, includes a botched story, a quotation taken
context, an evil deed made light of, a good event ig

Some of what we read, watch, and hear, it must b
ted, are merely careless bloopers. I have seen the
Association of Evangelicals mislabeled as "the Natio
ciation of Evangelists," for example. Newspapers a
magazines frequently misspell the word *Pentecosta*)·
tacostal" (a la "Pentagon," a far more familiar bea

> *Just when you think all positive mention of Christianity has been banned, you get surprised.*

When reporters refer to "the Reverend Chuck Colson" or "the Reverend James Dobson," they obviously haven't done their homework; neither man is ordained. (When the copy comes out "the Reverend James *Dodson*," insult is added to injury.) This kind of sloppiness is supposed to have been beaten out of writers back in Journalism 101.

But worse by far are the intentional maneuvers: the booby-trap questions, the unflattering photographs, the devious transitions, the sensationalized summaries. Some of these journalistic twists are indeed driven by the writer's animosity. But some have other origins. Journalists sometimes walk themselves into distortion by simply trying to be too clever or cute. Another motive is the ever-present thirst in mass media to be bold and shocking. Television news is infamous for its cavalier maxim "If it bleeds, it leads"—meaning that any story with dramatic footage of bloodshed goes to the top of the lineup. Some interviews can get bloody as well, and when they do, fairness is the casualty.

Not too many Christian parents these days are thrilled f their son or daughter shows interest in becoming a re- orter. Somehow it doesn't rank nearly as high as becoming doctor, a minister, a businessperson, or even an athlete. er all, polls have shown that many in the news media decidedly leftist opinions: To them, abortion is fine, sexuality is acceptable, and churchgoing is pointless. hristian colleges offer strong programs in journalism, erefore few Christian young people enter the field only extends the problem).

A *U.S. News & World Report* poll in 1995 showed that among Americans at large, the likes of Tom Brokaw and Peter Jennings were fairly unpopular. When voters were asked whether their personal goals conflicted with any of the following nine groups, the "yes" vote was fascinating:

With gun owners	36%
With elected officials	36%
With the National Rifle Association	39%
With large corporations	40%
With talk-radio hosts	41%
With lawyers	45%
With welfare recipients	49%
With prime-time TV	49%
With the news media	50%[1]

ENTIRELY CORRUPT?

It is not quite fair, however, to say that the newsroom has totally become Sodom. Just when you think all positive mention of Christianity has been banned, you get surprised. A case in point: On May 27, 1996, two weeks after the horrendous ValuJet crash in the alligator-infested Florida Everglades, most front pages carried the story of divers finally finding the cockpit voice recorder. The Associated Press version did not censor out the following explanation from Metro-Dade Police Sergeant Felix Jimenez: "When we stopped for a break, I said, 'God, so far I've just prayed for you to keep everyone safe out here and I haven't asked for your help finding anything. Now I'm asking you to help us find this recorder.' The next time I put my probe into the water, it hit the recorder."

Why wasn't the AP embarrassed to run that? Apparently the editors found it authentic and elected to leave it in the story, thus reminding millions of readers that prayer is not a joke.

This kind of thing belies the assumption among many conservative Christians that the news media are totally incorrigible, a lost tribe of apostates. When one ministry headquarters building was invaded by a gunman who wanted to settle a personal grudge by taking hostages, the local media naturally came to cover the story. The standoff lasted all afternoon, until the police finally talked the man into giving himself up. Mercifully, no one was injured or killed. In writing about this drama to the organization's supporters, a vice president expressed amazement at the fair and "respectful" reporting. "That the press covered the events in an even-handed manner was a miracle in itself," he wrote—as if the local journalists were by nature committed to distortion but must have forgotten this once.[2] What possible spin could have been dreamed up for this particular crime story? There was no controversial or political angle to exploit.

One cannot say that the tens of thousands of people who write the nation's news and feature stories all distort their articles any more than that all carpenters pad their billings or all used-car salesmen lie. We must be careful not to engage in blanket condemnation. As Tim Stafford once wrote, "Complaining about the news seems to be the equivalent of reviling camp food when you are in junior high."[3] While it feels good to spout off, it is not entirely honest to condemn the entire menu week after week.

In fact, we know that some of today's secular journalism is worthy by the fact that it gets quoted in the conservative Christian press. Christian leaders and editors enjoy citing editorials or statistics from *Newsweek*, the *Wall Street Journal*, or the *New York Times* if they happen to agree with the content, thus bolstering whatever argument they are making. So the press can't be all bad.

Once in a while, the news media are even recruited as an ally. Consider the rescue movement, which in the late

1980s and early 1990s drew huge attention to abortion by blocking the doorways of clinics where the unborn were killed. I was personally intrigued by this effort, to the point of participating myself one drizzly Saturday morning in October 1988. With more than a hundred others, I parked my six-foot-six-inch frame in front of the Summit Women's Center in downtown Bridgeport, Connecticut, and spent the next four hours quietly praying and singing. On the opposite sidewalk, the clinic managers fumed while the police (many of whom seemed to sympathize with our cause) took their time deciding what to do. It was close to noon before four of them finally picked me up by my shoulders and ankles, deposited me with others in the back of a postal van, and drove us down to the city jail, where we were processed, fingerprinted, and released. (In court a few weeks later, charges of "creating a public disturbance" were dropped for our whole group on a technicality.) Meanwhile, the goal was reached: No abortions took place that day at the Summit Women's Center. My wife went through the same experience four months later in our hometown of Danbury, Connecticut, with the same results.

Of the many things we learned on the rescue barricades (which would take a whole other chapter to articulate), one was this: The presence of television cameras and reporters with notepads made all the difference in the world. Had they not been present, the entire drama would have crumbled. The police, at the urging of the clinic owners, would have removed us in a matter of minutes, and that would have been that. The whole point was to make a *public* statement, to conduct a piece of street theater that would play well on the evening news. One of our group's main planners, in fact, was a former newspaperman who did not even attend the rescue. He stayed home by his telephone, briefing his media contacts all through the day on what was happening and what it meant. This was an important part of the strategy.

> *The more people know about what is really taking place, the better equipped they are to make intelligent decisions.*

In the years that followed, the media grew tired of rescue operation stories and the nation's police grew tired of wrenching their vertebrae. They clamped down on the drama, and judges got very tough in sentencing. The tactic thus lost some of its "newsworthiness." Most abortion opponents have since moved on to other strategies. But while rescues lasted, reporters were key players in the script. Their willingness to print dramatic photos of elderly nuns being handcuffed, to write profile stories about people making this personal sacrifice who otherwise never broke the law, were specimens of service to the conservative Christian agenda. They let the public know what was going on in this moral controversy.

INFORMATION FOR ALL

And so it should be in a free society. The more people know about what is really taking place, the better equipped they are to make intelligent decisions. That is why the founding fathers felt so strongly about freedom of the press. They had seen enough of royal censorship in Europe. They particularly watched France convulse in a terrible revolution where the masses had little idea of what was happening. In America, they were determined to open the news windows wide.

Can you believe Thomas Jefferson's bold statement in 1787?

> The basis of our government being the opinion of the people, the very first object should be to keep that

right, and were it left to me to decide whether we should have a government without newspapers, or newspapers without a government, I should not hesitate a moment to choose the latter.

Jefferson actually believed that if people knew the facts of the day and expressed their views about them, however subjective or eccentric, the culture would somehow get along better than if a government decided everything without outside scrutiny. People would have to solve their own problems and adjudicate their own debates somehow.

This faith in the value of a free and independent press is sorely lacking today. We have become so irritated with the news media's faults and biases that we have forgotten how bad life would become without them. Scandals would go unexposed, power would reign unchecked, and helpful new ideas would go unconsidered.

I freely confess that I don't *want* to know everything I read in the newspaper. But I *need* to know many of those things nonetheless. Citizens need information, even uncomfortable information. Without information, our ability to self-govern is stunted.

Jefferson's theory was at times put to severe testing. The press in his day could be vicious. When he ran for president in 1800, the *Gazette of the United States*, which was the newspaper of the Federalists (opposition party), accused him of "weaknesses of nerves, want of fortitude and total imbecility of character." Ouch! He won the election anyway. The diatribes continued, however, throughout Jefferson's first term, to the point that he could not resist a complaint in his second inaugural address in 1805:

> The artillery of the press has been levelled against us, charged with whatsoever its licentiousness could devise or dare. These abuses of an institution so important to freedom and science are deeply to be regretted,

inasmuch as they tend to lessen its usefulness, and to sap its safety.

But Jefferson's knees did not buckle. While he would use the bully pulpit to lecture the newspapers of his day toward more responsible behavior, he would not muffle them. They played too important a role in this democratic experiment called America. Long after he left office, in an 1816 letter to Charles Yancey, he wrote: "Where the press is free, and every man able to read, all is safe."

TRUTH WILL PREVAIL

Modern minds will perhaps find Jefferson too optimistic, too trusting. They will say that Americans today can't sort out truth from error, news facts from opinion, and thus are led down dark paths. But one has only to look at other nations where the press is tightly controlled to see the bitter fruit.

We are left with the job of advocating for truth on the basis of its own merit, not governmental decree. This makes for a noisy public square, because others are pitching their ideas too. If we want freedom for *Christianity Today* magazine, we will have to endure the Nation of Islam's *Final Call* being hawked on street corners. If we want political commentary from the right, we have to put up with political commentary from the left.

What about open distortion? What about "hatchet journalism"? What about insults aimed at Christian leaders today like those unleashed at Jefferson? Should a contemporary author be allowed to call Pat Robertson a "greedy ... power hungry and possibly megalomaniacal" man who "seeks to make the United States a fundamentalist Christian version of Iran with himself installed as chief ayatollah"?[4] Even *Publishers Weekly* called this book a "screed."

Well, there are legal boundaries. Federal law does not stretch so far as to protect defamation, obscenity, sedition, or treason, each of which has been defined in detail for court use. The definitions do not go as far as many of us would, from time to time, earnestly desire, but they are a start.

Outside of those criminal expressions, however, we are on our own to reason and debate as best we can. It does less good to lecture the other fellow on his unfairness than it does to prove him incorrect by diligent marshaling of the facts. When it comes to opinions, we must express ours in a tone of respect and tolerate our opponent's in the same vein.

> *We must express our opinions in a tone of respect and tolerate our opponent's in the same vein.*

Lifting up the value of hearing the other person's viewpoint and checking all the relevant facts is obvious wisdom, one would think—but in fact it needs constant repeating. Christians do not help their cause when they take journalistic shortcuts. How does one defend the attitude expressed by the publisher of a well-known Christian newsmagazine: "Readers are best served, I have found, if I decide very early in the process what I think the story should say. Then I deliberately look for details to back up my preconception."[5]

Say what?

No wonder he has found an editor, a talented journalist, who believes, "A solidly Christian news publication should not be balanced. It should fight a limited war against secular, liberal culture."[6] Perhaps he means only that his magazine is not intended to be neutral on moral issues. That is fine (and legal). But if he means that facts are subservient to dogma, then his readers are ill-served, and so is the general public.

The serene confidence of John Milton, brilliant English poet of the seventeenth century, is worth repeating in our turbulent cacophony of media output:

> Though all the winds of doctrine were let loose to play upon the earth, so [if] Truth be in the field, we do injuriously, by licensing and prohibiting, to misdoubt her strength. Let her and Falsehood grapple; who ever knew Truth put to the worse, in a free and open encounter?[7]

The apostle Paul wrote much the same thing in 1 Thessalonians 5:21–22. "Test everything. Hold on to the good. Avoid every kind of evil." There is much evil in the modern news media to avoid. But there is also some good. Every column, every interview, every sound bite must be tested to see if it enlightens, benefits, and educates, or if it demeans, distorts, and darkens. The media, after all, are merely the voices of human beings in a fallen society.

Jesus said: "Out of the overflow of the heart the mouth speaks [and writes and edits and broadcasts]. The good man brings good things out of the good stored up in him, and the evil man brings evil things out of the evil stored up in him" (Matt. 12:34–35). That is abundantly evident with regard to the news media. The more we bring the light of good thinking, good reporting, good writing, and good filming to the public square, the less time we will have—and the less need there will be—for complaint.

Ten

Where Often Is Heard a Discouraging Word

If you heard the following quotation and didn't catch who the speaker was, what would be your guess? Do these words sound like they come from the mouth of a twenty-two-year-old, a forty-two-year-old, or a sixty-two-year old?

> I don't understand what's going on in this messed-up world. There's nobody you can even respect anymore. The people who are supposed to be leading us are nothing but jerks. Everything's sliding downhill. People just look out for themselves these days and shaft the other guy without a thought. Who would be stupid enough to bring kids into a world like this?

Most listeners would attribute this kind of agitation to a young adult, a person without much experience who is struggling for a toehold in life. If all you have are a new diploma and a very short resume, it is normal to fall prey to worry and panic as employers turn you down, security guards look you over twice, and potential girlfriends or boyfriends brush you off.

Throughout the ages, it has been the task of older and wiser people to encourage the young, to hold them steady in moments of anxiety, to affirm their talents and bolster their shaky knees. Every young adult needs an older friend who quietly says, "The world isn't quite as berserk as it seems. In time you will find your place and even make a valuable contribution. Don't give up; don't give in to cynicism and fear. Here, let me help you...."

WHY GENERATION X IS DEPRESSED

Unfortunately, not many young people are getting that kind of help these days. Instead, the above complaint (with slightly different wording) is heard more frequently from the mouths of forty-two-year-olds and sixty-two-year-olds. The generations that have lived long enough to have gained perspective are the ones expressing the greatest dismay and discouragement. Journalists are now starting to dub them "the Anxious Class."

Robert Bork, eminent conservative jurist who almost made it onto the Supreme Court, entitled his new book *Slouching Towards Gomorrah*.[1] How inspiring! The religious publishing scene is not much better. One insightful observer had the courage to stand up in front of a Christian Booksellers Association convention and say, "We are dishing out more alarm than hope."[2] As a result, he noted, some conservative Christian families have grown so nervous about their children's moral environment that they have moved beyond home schooling to "home churching"—that is, keeping their kids out of Sunday school classes and church youth groups for fear they might be contaminated by less spiritual peers.

Read the mail that arrives from conservative Christian organizations; it is overwhelmingly dark in tone. Times are terrible, Satan is winning on all sides, the church is in disarray. The light at the end of the tunnel has been turned off.

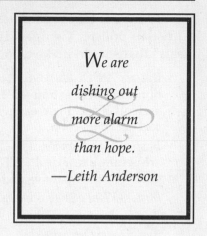

We are dishing out more alarm than hope.

—*Leith Anderson*

What does this kind of rhetoric say to a young person? It says that the elders are without hope or courage, and so one might as well give up. No wonder Generation X is "bummed" (to use their jargon). Much has been written about the sour mood of those born between the mid-1960s and the mid-1980s. They are said to be self-centered, disorganized, surly, and unmotivated ("slackers"). These Baby Busters, of course, point to a plethora of causes for their attitude (few good jobs, the national debt they'll have to try to pay off, weak parenting in their early years, divorced parents, a polluted ecosystem). But we cannot deny that they have picked up some of their gloom from us.

In the survey mentioned in chapter 5 that asked, "Do you think America's best years are behind us, or still ahead of us?" people in the fifteen-to-twenty-four age range said "behind" by a 54 percent to 37 percent margin. Clinical psychologist Joseph W. Ciarrocchi, who teaches at Loyola College in Maryland, writes that Generation X has "rates of depression ten times higher than those born in earlier generations in the United States. This has enormous pastoral implications."[3]

In his book *Baby Busters: The Disillusioned Generation*, Christian pollster George Barna lists ten "contours of the heart" that should make us ponder.

> *Busters Are Disillusioned.* More than any prior generation, they feel estranged from God, separated from each other, lacking meaning in life, void of roots and a societal connection. . . .
>
> *Busters Feel Abandoned.* . . . Many Busters believe they are getting a raw deal. . . . They resent having been forgotten by their parents and the older generations.
>
> *Busters Want a High Quality of Life.*
>
> *Busters Are Independent.*
>
> *Busters Are Defensive.*
>
> *Busters Are Comfortable with Change.*
>
> *Busters Are More Sensitive to People.*
>
> *Busters Are Pluralists.*
>
> *Busters Are Flexible.* There are few absolutes and few immovable standards in their lives.
>
> *Busters Are Pragmatic.* . . . Lacking a holistic sense of mission or a comprehensive world view, they cope on a situational basis.[4]

This explains why Baby Busters don't place a lot of stock in the labels "liberal" and "conservative."[5] They are far more interested in relationships than in categories. On their list of important elements in life, "family" gets the most votes (93 percent), followed by "health" (84 percent), "my time" (78 percent), and "my friends" (64 percent). "Money" comes far down the list (40 percent), and at the very bottom comes "government and politics" (26 percent).[6]

A Boston pastor to the Generation X crowd puts it succinctly when he says, "Busters aren't looking for programs providing nice experiences. Instead, they long for meaningful relationships, such as with older church members who can show them, for example, what a good marriage looks like."[7]

If church members and church leaders are consumed with culture battles fueled by harsh, antirelational words, they are not likely to be heard by the younger generation. Fighting doesn't appeal to them; they have already seen and heard enough conflict in their homes and schools while growing up. Even when important debates need their support, an inner reluctance says, *Do I really have to get involved with this?*

An articulate member of Generation X wrote to a conservative Christian ministry not long ago.

> I don't believe you fully appreciate the generational nature of the differences [being] discussed. There are a lot of young Evangelicals like myself who care passionately about their country, but are simply not motivated by the limited agenda and apocalyptic tone. . . . Maybe my generation has been raised to tolerate too much, but we have a greater desire to see a society that can live together. . . . Folks in my age group react very poorly to the pushy, authoritative tone of Christian Right leaders. Most importantly, we don't want to fight scared; we want to fight smart.

A GREAT NEED TO LEAD

The mantle of leadership falls slowly and silently upon everyone's shoulders with the passing of time. Even in our late thirties, younger people are starting to look up to us, and by the time we reach our forties, young eyes are watching us carefully, wanting to see how a successful and coherent adulthood is built. We may think, *Who, me? I'm not a role model to anyone.* But that is untrue. The generation behind us is constantly checking us out.

They try to be cool about it; they don't often put their questions into words. But they are thinking nonetheless:

How do you build a marriage that lasts?

How do you manage money?

How do you connect with a non-Christian society?

How do you navigate ethical dilemmas in the
    workplace?
How do you raise healthy kids?
How do you connect with God?

This is why there is, and always has been, a desperate
need for voices like that of the elderly Moses, who said to
Joshua in front of the entire nation of Israel, "Be strong and
courageous, for you must go with this people into the
land. . . . The LORD himself goes before you and will be with
you; he will never leave you nor forsake you. Do not be
afraid; do not be discouraged" (Deut. 31:7–8). What a vote
of confidence for a younger man facing a huge challenge!

Where today are the godly fathers like David, who
from his deathbed inspired his son Solomon, "Be strong,
show yourself a man, and observe what the LORD your God
requires . . . so that you may prosper in all you do and wherever you go" (1 Kings 2:2–3). "The LORD be with you, and
may you have success and build the house of the LORD your
God, as he said you would. May the LORD give you discre-
tion and understanding when he puts you in command over
Israel. . . . Be strong and courageous. Do not be afraid or discouraged" (1 Chron. 22:11–13).

Where are the modern Pauls who will say with assur-
ance to the young, insecure Timothys of our time, "We have
put our hope in the living God, who is the Savior of all men,
and especially of those who believe. Command and teach
these things. Don't let anyone look down on you because
you are young, but set an example for the believers in speech,
in life, in love, in faith and in purity" (1 Tim. 4:10–12).

Listen to the positive tone in 2 Timothy 1:2–4. "My dear
son: . . . I thank God . . . as night and day I constantly remember you in my prayers. . . . I long to see you, so that I may be
filled with joy." Both epistles convey a message of *You can do
it, Timothy! You can advance God's kingdom in the midst of a
troubled world, and I'll show you how.* What a stark contrast to

the message sent all too often today that says, *The culture is in a moral free fall, and you young people don't even care. In fact, your generation is a major part of the problem, with all your promiscuity, your drugs, your pleasure-seeking, your slacking off. America is in big trouble now, and you don't even "get it."*

Leadership requires a higher, more informed outlook than that. It focuses on solution rather than blame, inspiration rather than accusation. It sorts out the contradictory claims—

> *Leadership focuses on solution rather than blame, inspiration rather than accusation.*

for example, the notion in the 1980s that Christian voters in America were a sleeping giant that could win any political battle if they would just wake up and put their muscle into it, followed by exactly the opposite notion in the 1990s: We're a poor, persecuted minority being picked on by a horde of terrible, ungodly Goliaths. Well, which is it? The Baby Busters don't know. They look to their elders to explain what is really happening, to sift out reality from mythology.

Os Guinness spotlights this contradiction in his excellent book *The American Hour:* "The present situation is reminiscent of the 1920s quip about a fundamentalist being someone who 'talks of standing on the rock of ages, but acts as if he were clinging to the last piece of driftwood.'"[8] Generation X picks up very quickly on this kind of incongruity and asks, "So, like, what's *really* going on?"

Real leaders must be willing to point out the good news of our time even though it doesn't support a gloom-and-doom paradigm. Here are some samples of information that Baby Busters desperately need to hear:

> *Even the Independent Majority is doing some things right, perhaps sometimes by accident, but sometimes by intent.*

• *The annual divorce rate is not one out of two—not even close.* It is rather one out of fifty. Says pollster Louis Harris, "The idea that half of American marriages are doomed is one of the most specious pieces of statistical nonsense ever perpetuated in modern times."[9] Think about it. On the street where you live, is every second home on the block breaking up? Hardly. Out of the approximately 55 million American marriages in existence today, 1.2 million will end in divorce this year—a tragedy for those households, to be sure. But meanwhile, the other 53.8 million marriages "just keep flowing along like Ol' Man River," notes Harris. The one-in-two superstition arose by comparing 1.2 million divorces in a year with 2.4 million weddings in a year. But the couples getting divorced are not the same couples who just got married; the two numbers have almost no direct link to one another. So here is an important message to Generation X: Don't be afraid of getting married! You can make a go of it—especially if you put God at the center of your relationship.

• *Not everyone is sleeping around.* Despite what you hear in popular music and on TV sitcoms, serious research shows a high degree of fidelity. The massive 1994 "Sex in America" study by the University of Chicago's National Opinion Research Center showed that 83 percent of Americans slept with only one person or else none in the course of a year. That leaves just 17 percent who were promiscuous. (The same survey, by the way, showed that the homosexual population is nowhere near the "10 percent" often quoted. It's 2.8 percent of men and 1.4 percent of women.)[10]

• *Many people are raising their children together.* According to the Population Reference Bureau, the number of two-parent homes with children increased by 700,000 in the years 1990 through 1995, reversing a twenty-year decline.[11]

• *Today's parents are not gone all the time.* The oft-repeated statistic that in only twenty years, parent-child interaction plunged 40 percent (from thirty hours a week to just seventeen) turned out to be bogus. The University of Maryland sociologist's research had a number of flaws in it.[12] He now says nobody knows for sure. While some modern parents are admittedly career-obsessed to the detriment of their kids, others are using flextime, job sharing, and work-at-home arrangements in ever more creative ways to be close to their growing sons and daughters.

• *Home ownership is not an impossible dream.* In 1996, the percentage of Americans who were buying their own homes was at its highest level in fifteen years. Mortgage rates were deliciously low. So was inflation.

• *You're less likely to get robbed, assaulted, raped, or murdered than you were a few years ago.* The annual total of all violent crimes started coming down in 1994 and dropped by another 9 percent in 1995, the Bureau of Justice Statistics reported.[13]

These are just a few of the reasons not to be totally depressed in our contemporary world. Even the Independent Majority is doing some things right, perhaps sometimes by accident, but sometimes by intent. Meanwhile, God has not lost his grip. In fact, he is eagerly on the hunt for Generation Xers and anyone else who will pursue his purposes in the contemporary climate.

I love the story of the Kansas farmer who went out with his combine one hot June day to bring in the winter wheat harvest. He had been watching his crop carefully ever since he had planted it the preceding October. The snows had come and gone and the green stalks had risen taller and taller throughout the spring and then had turned golden in the summer heat.

He pulled into this quarter-section of land, revved his engine, set his sights on a telephone pole on the horizon, and began to reap the first swath. He looked forward to reaching the end of the field, where he would make a right-hand turn and continue along the fence on the second side, eventually completing the outer rectangle, and so on.

Ten minutes later he found it odd that no fence had yet appeared in front of him. He kept going. In another few minutes, he knew something was definitely wrong. He stopped, took the engine out of gear, and stood up to look behind him. There the path of cut wheat was not straight at all. It meandered here and there, curving this way and that. The farmer had somehow managed to chop up his field in a completely inefficient pattern.

He looked forward again for the marker toward which he had been steering and only then realized it was not a telephone pole at all, but rather the moving smokestack of his neighbor's tractor in the adjoining field!

If we steer our course according to what Washington is doing or how the mass media are moving, we will only make a mess of things. Soon we will find ourselves wasting time and gasoline. But if we keep our eye on the marker that does not move—the cross of Christ—we will make steady progress in the right direction. Confusion and discouragement will not overwhelm us. And the young generation that follows in our tracks will have a reliable example to follow.

Part Three

What Doth the Lord Require?

And now you have an extraordinary opportunity, a day wherein Christ has thrown the door of mercy wide open.

Jonathan Edwards
"Sinners in the Hands of an Angry God," 1741

Eleven

Greater Is He

If we are ever to regain our balance in these unsettling times, if we are ever to move beyond hand-wringing and frustration, the place to begin is with the size and kind of God we serve. And for that information, let me suggest a most unlikely source: the hymnal!

A huge gap exists between the way many Christians think today and the way they sing. While their minds are obsessed with anxiety and consternation over the culture war, they stand in church every seventh day and boldly proclaim the stalwart lyrics of classic hymns such as

"Eternal Father, Strong to Save"
"A Mighty Fortress Is Our God"

"Come, Thou Almighty King"
"Great Is Thy Faithfulness"
"Praise to the Lord, the Almighty"
"How Great Thou Art"
"God Will Take Care of You"
"The Lord's My Shepherd"

Mixed in with these classics (or in some churches, re-placing them) are contemporary choruses with lyrics such as

"How majestic is your name"
"Our God is an awesome God"
"He is able, more than able"
"Great is the Lord"
"Jesus, your name is power"
"Great and mighty is he"
"If God be for us, who can be against us?"
"Our God reigns"
"He is Lord"
"What a mighty God we serve"
"Jesus, name above all names"
"Holy, holy, holy, Lord God of power and might"
"Greater is he that is in me"

Either the songwriters of the past and present are a bunch of wild-eyed optimists, or else they are tapping into bedrock truth that many of us have forgotten. I suspect the latter. Most of these lyrics are half Scripture anyway, show-ing that the lyricists' confidence springs not from their own minds but from the Book they've been reading.

The final chorus in the above list traces back to the apostle John's first epistle. After talking frankly about all the false prophets in the world, "the spirit of the antichrist," and other dangers of his time, he rebounds with this ringing dec-laration: "You, dear children, are from God and have over-come them, because the one who is in you is greater than the one who is in the world" (1 John 4:4).

Do we truly believe this? Are we convinced that our Lord is fundamentally stronger than the devil and his followers? If so, then why all the dismay? Should not a great, almighty God be able to handle the local five-member school curriculum committee, for example, or a panel of nine black-robed judges?

John's statement is almost a direct echo of something Elisha said nine hundred years earlier in the midst of a showdown with the Aramean army. He and his servant found themselves trapped in the city of Dothan. Early in the morning, the servant went outside and panicked at the sight of horses and chariots on every side of town. God's representatives were surely about to be massacred. He ran in terror to the prophet.

> *Are we convinced that our Lord is fundamentally stronger than the devil . . . ? If so, then why all the dismay?*

Did Elisha share his panic? Did he start looking for a human solution: a scheme to escape, perhaps, or an appeal to the outside world for armies to come save them? Not at all.

> "Don't be afraid," the prophet answered. "Those who are with us are more than those who are with them."
>
> And Elisha prayed, "O LORD, open his eyes so he may see." Then the LORD opened the servant's eyes, and he looked and saw the hills full of horses and chariots of fire all around Elisha (2 Kings 6:16–17).

In our time of attack and counterattack, we desperately need our eyes to be opened to the supernatural dimension. That will give us confidence to call for *God's* intervention when enemies move forward, just as Elisha prayed for the Arameans to be struck blind. In a matter of minutes, the whole scene changed, and Elisha was firmly in control of his enemies. He took them on a little march straight to Samaria and handed them over to the Israelite military!

Surely God is alert to the threats we face in modern America, the opponents of all that he has marked as his own. He has our situation under constant surveillance and is prepared to act with overwhelming force if necessary. Not everyone sees God's heavenly legions at the moment—but we, of all people, should see them. We are far from alone.

Some friends of mine named Derek and Judy lived in a Chicago suburb that was hit one September with a nasty school strike. The administration and the teachers' union had negotiated throughout the summer without success. The day came for classes to begin; neither side budged. Parents thought a contract would surely be hammered out in a day or two, but the strike dragged on through the first week of the semester and well into the second.

Derek and Judy's children were not directly affected— they attended a Christian school—but the family couldn't help noticing the unfortunate scene at the public elementary school a few blocks from their home: teachers on the picket line, looking a little sheepish as they carried their signs, and bewildered children standing across the street watching, wondering, remembering how they had always looked up to their kind and wise teachers as role models, but now the grown-ups were arguing and fighting.... *Why, Mom? Will I ever get to go back to school?*

One evening Judy said with some agitation to her husband, "This is really getting ugly, Derek. It's not just a money problem; the whole community is upset, and we're all setting a terrible example for kids. Who's doing anything about this? How long is this going to go on? Why doesn't the church step in? They ought to at least call a special prayer meeting or something."

"Well, yes," Derek replied. "But since you mentioned it, how much prayer have you and I put into this problem?" They both knew the answer to that one.

A couple of hours later, after darkness had fallen, Derek suggested that they go for a walk. They made their way through the shadowy streets down to the school corner, now quiet after another day of picketing. The building was locked, of course, but the two of them sat at one of the kid-sized picnic tables and, while crickets chirped in the distance, they prayed.

"Dear God, this situation is a mess. Nothing good is coming out of this; everybody is a loser here, if not financially, then in terms of respect. The kids of our community aren't getting to learn, and the adults are just getting angrier and angrier with each other. We don't know how to solve this—but can you please help? Bring peace to our town somehow. . . ."

They prayed for maybe half an hour and then quietly walked home.

The next morning the clock radio came on as usual at 6:00 A.M. Derek and Judy were gradually edging toward consciousness when they heard the announcer say, ". . . partly cloudy today, with a high this afternoon in the upper seventies. . . . There's been a settlement overnight in the District 200 school strike. Teachers will be back in the classrooms today, and students are to report at the usual time."

What! So quickly? The couple sat up in bed and stared at each other, gasping. The strike was over! How did that happen?

Derek told me later, "I'm not nearly presumptuous enough to claim that our little prayers there on the playground turned the tide. Don't ask me to explain all the dynamics here—all I know is that a complicated tangle of human strife

> *Christians often recognize God's work in small details of life but forget his larger designs.*
>
> —Fisher Humphreys

was suddenly resolved, and I think God had something to do with it."

Theologian Fisher Humphreys has written, "Although our world today is very chaotic, I do not believe that it has slipped out of God's control. He is using it to do what he intended.... Christians often recognize God's work in small details of life but forget his larger designs."[1]

NOT ALONE AFTER ALL

More than a century after Elisha's time, his phrase was repeated by King Hezekiah in the midst of terrible danger from the Assyrians. Their threats were real; they had already conquered the northern ten tribes of Israel and were now headed south to wipe out Judah as well. Listen to Hezekiah's bold statement at a public gathering: "Be strong and courageous. Do not be afraid or discouraged because of the king of Assyria and the vast army with him, for *there is a greater power with us than with him.* With him is only the arm of flesh, but with us is the LORD our God to help us and to fight our battles" (2 Chron. 32:7–8, italics added). Once again, as in Elisha's case, the pagan army was rebuffed and God's people spared from devastation.

In the conflicts we face today in a self-centered, highly irreligious society, who knows what God might do if we truly expect him to act? Unfortunately, we have too often sunk to the deistic assumptions described in chapter 4: God is far away now, or dozing, or shriveled up with old age, and we have to fight these battles alone. Such a view leads straight to exhaustion.

We are like the disciples trying to row across Lake Galilee in pitch darkness, the headwinds topping twenty knots, the howling gale striking terror in our hearts. We are pulling for all we're worth, sweat pouring off our bodies. We are soaked with the spray of the waves and are starting to growl at the others in the boat for not working as hard as we are to stave off disaster. The squall intensifies, and in the pit of our stomachs, we fear we shall never see land again.

There is one person in the boat who is not frantic, however. He is so composed that he's asleep. His name is Jesus. His power and authority are immediately available. He's not removed, aloof, or uncaring about our plight. He waits to be asked.

Christians of all ages have made the mistake of feeling that Jesus is close to us on sunny days when the water is calm and we're paddling successfully toward our goal, but that he is far away when the waves are crashing upon us and we're making no headway. We know better, of course, but we forget. If we think Jesus is not in our boat at such a time, maybe it is because he's not screaming like we are. His quietness goes unnoticed amid our shouts. This does not at all change the fact of who he is and what he can do. One word from his lips, and the storm will change in short order.

Greater is he who is in our boat than all the cultural northeasters.

IS GOD "SLOW"?

Of course, we cannot guarantee that God will see every threat the way we see it. No doubt there will come some nights when we plead with God to act and he elects not to get involved because he sees the conflict differently.

Perhaps what we consider to be evil is instead, to his way of thinking, merely neutral.

Or perhaps he would like to intervene but cannot due to his great respect for human freedom. If he reached down

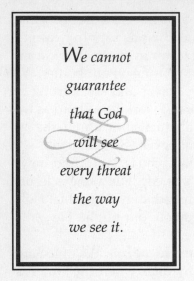

We cannot guarantee that God will see every threat the way we see it.

and torpedoed the pornographer's business, for example, he would thereby be forcing that person to live God's way whether he wanted to or not. All the way back to the Garden of Eden, God has allowed tempting trees and smooth-talking serpents to grow up close to the human beings he has made—and has been willing to live with the consequences.

Or perhaps God is planning a more long-range response that will achieve three or four of his goals simultaneously.

In his book *Uncommon Decency*, Richard J. Mouw closes with a chapter entitled "Serving a Slow God." Without meaning any disrespect, he shows how God often moves at a slower pace than we would like. This exasperates us sometimes. We want him to hurry up, to cure all ills, to settle all scores. When he does not, we often conclude that he doesn't really care, and so we'll have to take up the job he is neglecting. Mouw writes:

> The Mennonites have a nice phrase that is helpful here. They say that we are living "in the time of God's patience." For God's own good reasons he has not yet ushered in the eternal kingdom. God is presently showing patience toward the human race, providing the unsaved with the opportunity to repent and the saved with the opportunity to learn the ways of obedience.[2]

Whether fast or slow, dramatic or subtle, God's action in this messy world should never be undersold. He is still the supreme authority, and while his timing may mystify us, his power is not to be doubted.

Of all the hymns that illuminate God and serve to correct our perspective, my favorite has become Maltbie D. Babcock's "This Is My Father's World." The first two stanzas are deceptively simple, merely celebrating the beauties "of rocks and trees, of skies and seas . . . in the rustling grass, I hear Him pass. . . ." Babcock was an outstanding athlete and student in college before becoming a minister, and he would often tell his secretary as he left the office for a two-mile run along the shores of Lake Ontario, "I'm going out to see my Father's world!"

One can easily dismiss this hymn, published in 1901, as nothing more than a paean to nature. But consider the third stanza (emphasis added):

> *This is my Father's world,*
> *O let me ne'er forget*
> That though the wrong seems oft so strong,
> God is the Ruler yet.
> *This is my Father's world:*
> *The battle is not done;*
> *Jesus who died shall be satisfied,*
> *And earth and heav'n be one.*

What kind of "wrong" could possibly have been strong back in 1901? Wasn't that the Victorian age, a lovely time of gaslight and petticoats, before society began to putrefy?

Actually, no. In 1901, America was embroiled in an ugly and highly unpopular guerrilla conflict in the faraway Philippines, a territory we had recently acquired (along with Puerto Rico and Guam) by winning the lopsided Spanish-American War. Parents wondered why their sons were being sent eight thousand miles across the Pacific to die in tropical jungles. This was, in an uncanny way, that period's equivalent to the Vietnam conflict.

And on September 6 of that year, a man with a large handkerchief wrapped around his hand like a bandage walked up to President William McKinley at a reception in Buffalo, New York. Concealed inside the handkerchief was a 32-caliber revolver. He shot the president twice at point-blank range. The nation held its breath for the next week as McKinley struggled for life—and then lost the fight.

Social turmoil was a reality when this hymn was written, just as it is today. But that did not change the fact that, in the greater view, the world remained in the hands of a heavenly Father whose love, wisdom, patience, and power were unshaken. He knew what he was doing then as he does now. He also knew what he was *allowing*. He held a clear gauge within himself of just how much human nonsense he would tolerate. And his plan for the end of time, when every knee shall bow and every tongue confess his lordship, remained firmly in place.

Has anything changed in a hundred years?

Twelve

How to Truly Change a Culture

One would assume that an almighty ruler such as we met in the last chapter would have a massive, overwhelming "ground force" here on earth to advance his will. Decrees made in heaven would be carried out by the King's agents in this world. Any opposition to the heavenly monarch would be swiftly and vigorously squelched.

That's what the medieval Crusaders thought.

But after all this time, we remain a Christ-following *Minority*. Apparently God has a different strategy in mind. If he indeed were upset with us for not having conquered the globe, he would have fired us long ago. The fact that he continues to work with us and even love us shows his

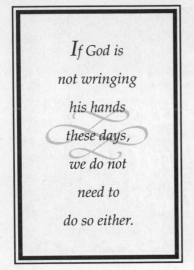

If God is not wringing his hands these days, we do not need to do so either.

willingness to take the slow route in improving this planet. While occasionally he will act dramatically on his own, most of the time he is quietly collaborating with us to bring his light to a dark culture.

Given our present state, especially in North America at the end of one century and the beginning of another, how do we make headway in Jesus' name? How do we advance God's priorities in ways that make him proud?

In this chapter we will look at five tactics for the minority as we seek to be God's people in a messy world.

1. CALM DOWN

If God is not wringing his hands these days, we do not need to do so either. If heaven is not in a state of depression, then neither should heaven's future residents be depressed. Besides, the watching majority is hardly attracted to such a mind-set.

Note that "Calm down" is not the same thing as "Go to sleep" or "Do nothing." It is rather the advice a volleyball coach gives to his or her players when they are so pumped up that they are running into each other, trying to spike every ball within reach instead of setting up, and are slamming balls out of bounds. What the coach means is *Control your adrenaline. Don't just flail around; make every move count.*

I remember visiting a few years ago the headquarters of a parachurch organization dedicated to fighting the culture war. A hostess took me on a tour of the offices and introduced me to various staff members. In one room, I shook hands with a man who told how a prominent Republican senator was now waffling on the issue of homosexuals in the military, and so the staffer was busy generating pressure to get him back in line. In the next office, I heard about an outrageous court decision in California on the rights of drug users. In a third office, I met someone feverishly trying to get Congress to reduce taxes.

The whole place seemed to be hyperventilating as people battled one cultural evil after another. I even caught myself breathing faster after about forty minutes! My blood seemed to be racing right along with theirs. *What must it be like to work here every day?* I wondered. It was a relief at the end of the tour to walk outside into the warm sunshine and take a slow breath.

Shortly after that, I read a biography of Amy Carmichael, the Irish missionary who went to southern India in 1895 and gave the rest of her life—fifty-five years—to rescuing children from sexual abuse in the Hindu temples. Parents of little girls, who viewed them as a financial liability anyway, were handing them over to the gods as early as age five. What that meant for a girl was a childhood as the priests' personal prostitute. Later on she would be made available to male pilgrims, who viewed sex with children as especially thrilling. By the time she reached her early teen years, she was used up and often diseased, so that the temple dismissed her into the streets to join a small caste called the *devadassis*, "prostitutes of the gods."

Amy Carmichael was duly aghast at this atrocity and set about to open an orphanage called the Dohnavur Fellowship. There many hundreds of young girls, and later boys, were sheltered from abuse and brought up in a loving and safe environment.

What was it like to wage this battle against a monstrous and well-entrenched evil? How did Amy Carmichael and her colleagues keep their sanity year after year as they saw

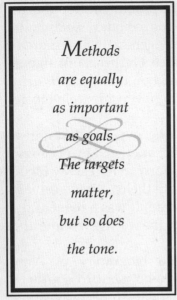

Methods are equally as important as goals. The targets matter, but so does the tone.

innocent little children being thrown to the most deviant sexual desecration?

Those who knew the missionary group said that they were remarkably calm. While they seriously disagreed with the majority practice in that culture, they conducted themselves in a way that gained respect. They particularly watched their words, being careful to speak evil of no one. Amy Carmichael herself wrote:

> As to others, we made one careful rule: the absent must be safe with us. Criticism, therefore, was taboo. . . . What other way of life could satisfy the heart that was set on living in the ungrieved presence of its Lord? The very thought of Him shames unkindness. It cannot abide before His clear countenance. . . . Lord, evermore give us this love.[1]

In her famous little book entitled *If*, which is a collection of short sayings, she wrote:

> If I can enjoy a joke at the expense of another; if I can in any way slight another in conversation, or even in thought, then I know nothing of Calvary love.
>
> If I can write an unkind letter, speak an unkind word, think an unkind thought without grief or shame, then I know nothing of Calvary love.[2]

Amy Carmichael's biographer tells about interviewing Eileen Kuhn, a missionary to Thailand who once visited the Dohnavur Fellowship. "I asked her for her most distinct impression. She had an immediate answer: peace. One could not pay a higher compliment to a work."[3]

That such a climate could be maintained in the face of overwhelming vice is a powerful example to us. It says that culture warfare does not need to inflame our spirits. It says that methods are equally as important as goals. The targets matter, but so does the tone. To win a battle through intimidation and sarcasm is not the victory we often think it is.

David wrote in Psalm 131:

> *I have stilled and quieted my soul;*
>   *like a weaned child with its mother,*
>   *like a weaned child is my soul within me.*
> *O Israel, put your hope in the LORD*
>   *both now and forevermore (vv. 2–3).*

A baby not yet weaned is often fretful, clamoring to be fed. A weaned child, by contrast, is more relaxed and at peace. He or she knows that the parent won't forget. Needs will be fulfilled at the proper time.

Culture warriors would do well, like David, to tell their souls from time to time, "Shhh . . . be still. Your hope is in the Lord, and he hasn't moved his throne half an inch." Such an attitude will benefit not only that person, but will, in a pragmatic way, make a better impression on opponents.

Agitated activists often do not realize how they defeat their own causes with their rhetoric simply because listeners are turned off. Popular talk-show host Larry King wrote in his newspaper column a week before the 1996 election "about how lucky President Clinton was to have four standout enemies, whose daily harangues actually benefit him. When you knock someone all the time, day in, day out, you, in effect, begin to preach only to the choir, while at the same time creating tremendous enthusiasm from everyone else." He then went on to name the four critics, two of whom are evangelical Christians. "The vitriol makes them tough to take, from silly rumors to incredible judgments to hearsay evidence. . . . The president ought to thank his lucky stars for all four. With enemies like these guys, you don't need friends."[4]

A phrase sticks in my memory from a few years back at our house, when my wife and I were in the thick of raising three young teenagers. They used to exhort each other sometimes when emotions would rise and an argument was about to break out: "Hey, calm your hormones!" It wasn't exactly a polite retort, but it did contain an element of wisdom. Sometimes in the fury of the culture war, we can act like impetuous junior-highers. A more cool-headed approach stands a better chance of winning the day—and honoring the Lord.

2. MAJOR ON THE MAJORS

Of all the improvements God would like to see in our world, which ones are at the top of his list? In a similar vein, which ones hold out the most promise to affect the most people?

No one can answer these questions for sure, but I doubt many of us would argue with placing *the salvation of individuals* at the pinnacle. To bring a person into a forgiven relationship with God is the greatest favor we could ever do for that person, not to mention his or her family, neighborhood, city, and nation. As Charles Colson puts it, "You don't change a culture by passing laws. You change a culture by changing people's habits. That's why the Gospel is so central to the possibilities of cultural reformation in American life."[5]

Anything that gets in the way of someone truly understanding and evaluating the gospel of Jesus Christ deserves a serious review. When Americans can't seem to hear the Good News because of the Christian media's stream of bad news delivered with acrimonious passion, something is terribly wrong.

Right beneath the goal of individual salvation must come the goal of *church planting*—establishing more and more places of nurture and teaching for those who have yielded to Christ. The Great Commission puts these two goals clearly in just a very few words: "Go and make disciples ..., teaching them" (Matt. 28:19–20).

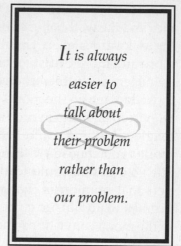

It is always easier to talk about their problem rather than our problem.

Once we broaden the scope to look at affecting the culture in general, what takes priority? William Bennett, former drug czar and well-known author of *The Book of Virtues*, among other writings, raised some eyebrows when he said to a conference of Christian conservatives, "I understand the aversion to homosexuality.... But if you look in terms of the damage to the children of America, you cannot compare what the homosexual movement, the gay rights movement, has done with what divorce has done to this society."[6] Bennett certainly did not mean to condone homosexual practice, which he views as immoral. All he was saying was, *Which problem is hurting our country more?*

Shortly after Cobb County, Georgia, passed an antigay resolution, David Boaz of the Cato Institute wrote in an editorial for the *New York Times*, "Surely, the 1,545 unwed mothers and the 2,739 divorcing couples created more social problems in the county than the 300 gay men and women who showed up at a picnic to protest [the resolution]."[7]

It is always easier for us to talk about *their* problem rather than *our* problem. When we don't know very many homosexuals, it is easy to wax eloquent against their wrongdoing. Meanwhile, speaking out against divorce and infidelity among us heterosexuals strikes closer to home. It makes people squirm in every church sanctuary. Ministers and laity alike have trouble summoning the courage to address these issues. But if we care about the health of families and the well-being of the next generation, we will break the awkward silence. Thankfully, that is happening today in more and more Christian circles.

Here is another choice we face: Who is wreaking the most damage on the moral fiber of our society—politicians, television and movie producers, or musicians? If you had a magic wand and could instantly reform one power center, would you choose Washington, Hollywood, or Nashville? Such a question could lead to lively debate, I suppose. My personal opinion is that the entertainment barons (both visual and audio) are currently making a much bigger dent in the moral convictions and behavior of Americans than are government officials. Yet who gets more of our protest?

We complain loudly, even to some fairly convoluted extremes, about laws that clash with our belief system. I remember one Christian group criticizing a federal requirement for higher gasoline efficiencies in vehicles on the grounds that it was "antifamily"—it might discourage Detroit from continuing to make minivans needed by households with several kids! Meanwhile, how seriously are we controlling the nightly flood of immoral sitcoms those children watch once they get out of the van and plop down in front of the television set? I am not saying that the political scene is unimportant. I am merely calling for a greater sense of perspective.

Minorities usually cannot afford to fight all battles at once. Therefore, they should deploy their limited resources and energy to the most urgent fronts.

3. APPRECIATE THE DIFFERENCE BETWEEN STATUTE AND STIGMA

Garry Wills once wrote an essay for *Time* magazine entitled "In Praise of Censure."[8] Wills's main point was that not everything bad in a society needs to be illegal; some of it can be controlled by giving it a bad reputation. Censure is not the same as *censoring*, which is an official act to prevent something from being published or aired. *Censure* is simply an effort to put a stigma on something, to say, "We don't like that. It's nasty and disgusting. Yes, you have a right to do it, but you won't win any popularity contests."

For a classic example in America, think of what has happened to smoking over the past thirty years. A practice that used to be acceptable and even debonair has, in just three short decades, become the opposite. When we watch an old movie today, we are jarred to see cigarettes in the hands of half the actors during what may otherwise be a wholesome and perhaps even goody-goody plot. If we travel abroad, we recoil the minute we step off the plane into the smoke-filled terminal at Amsterdam or Frankfurt or Tokyo, thinking, *This feels like the olden days in America.*

In those years gone by, conservative Christians preached against tobacco on moral grounds, that it was a pollution of the body God had created—an entirely valid point. But the preaching wasn't all that effective in changing the Independent Majority's habits. Instead, medical evidence began to come to light, leading to a warning from the U.S. surgeon general, and little by little, the culture began to change its mind. Nonsmoking areas began to pop up in restaurants and airplanes, then office buildings. The power of stigma was taking hold.

What other behaviors might be curbed through the same tactic?

A billboard campaign against obscenity a few years ago in several cities is a good example. Located as close to the sleaze shops as possible, huge signs featured celebrity faces and the bold slogan "Real Men Don't Use Porn." Nothing was said about taking legal action to *censor* the smut, to bring the force of government against the pornographers (although present law does provide for that). The billboards merely engaged in *censure,* an informal disapproval of this degrading material.

On the abortion front, there is evidence that more headway is being made among physicians by stigmatizing the procedure than will ever be made in the halls of Congress. Younger doctors especially are saying "no thanks" to the practice. Dr. Warren Hern, who performs abortions in Boulder, Colorado, told a *New York Times* reporter that he and others like him "are treated as a pariah by the medical community. At best, we are tolerated." Dr. Joseph S. Randall, an Atlanta gynecologist who stopped doing abortions after his spiritual conversion, told the same reporter, "Other doctors treated us as second-class M.D.s."[9]

For a minority group such as Christ-followers, the tactic of well-planned and carefully executed stigmatizing offers especially bright promise.

4. KEEP LOOKING FOR ALLIES

Once again we encounter an admonition that is just common sense when you're outnumbered. If you lack the votes to propel your values to the top, you're smart to make common cause with other people, even those who might disagree with you on half a dozen other items.

U.S. Senator John Ashcroft, an Assemblies of God layman, tells about a time during his days as governor of Missouri when he chaired the Education Commission of the States. Here he sat at a conference table with national leaders of all different persuasions trying to craft recommendations on a subject so volatile as public schooling. Had Ashcroft stumped for a resolution on prayer and Bible reading, he would immediately have been attacked for trying to interject his religion into the debate. Had he launched a volley against sex education, the room would have erupted in conflict. Instead, he wisely suggested a list of values that might be good to stress in American schools, things such as:

- It's better to build something than to tear something down.
- It's better to earn something than to steal something.
- It's better to be independent than to be dependent.
- It's better to tell the truth than to tell a lie.
- It's better to be on time than to be late.
- It's better to rely on facts than on prejudice.
- Families are better than promiscuity.[10]

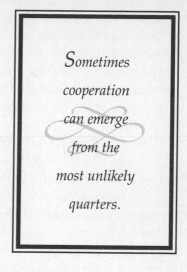

Sometimes cooperation can emerge from the most unlikely quarters.

Naturally, Ashcroft won a lot of allies that day. Who could argue that the nation's schools would not be better places for carrying these kinds of messages? While such precepts fall short of actually guiding a student to faith in Jesus Christ, neither can we claim that the rote classroom prayers of years gone by were all that effective, either.

Sometimes cooperation can emerge from the most unlikely quarters. Monnica Terwilliger, a volunteer at Los Angeles's Westside Crisis Pregnancy Center, got the naive notion in 1996 to ask nearby abortion clinics for referrals of any clients who were uncertain about ending their pregnancies. "I've always thought that people who consider themselves pro-choice should support crisis pregnancy centers," she says. "So I suggested we write letters inviting abortion clinics to send women ambivalent about abortion to us."

How foolish, many Christians would say. Didn't Monnica know that abortion counselors are rock-solid against any option but their own? Her letters were sure to be met with scorn and derision.

Well, as a matter of fact, one week after the ten letters went into the mail, the first confused teenager showed up at Westside's door saying that the abortion clinic across the street had sent her over. Four more arrived in the next few days, from two different clinics. The happily surprised Westside bosses decided to repeat the mailings every six weeks for a while.[11]

So much for the stereotype of pro-abortionists.

Is not this the tactic the apostle Paul used in wending his way through a complex world? In Acts 23 we see him co-opting the Pharisees during a court trial, citing their common belief in bodily resurrection and thus getting them to defend him, even though on many other occasions they despised him. In Acts 24 he freely complimented the Roman governor Felix's knowledge of religious law. In Acts 26 he did the same with King Herod Agrippa. Aboard ship in Acts 27, he shared critical insights with a Roman centurion during a hurricane-force storm on the Mediterranean, thus preventing loss of life.

None of these men were particularly godly. But every one of them went away respecting Paul for his character and reasonableness. Paul explained, "Though I am free and belong to no man, I make myself a slave to everyone, to win as many as possible.... I have become all things to all men so that by all possible means I might save some. I do all this for the sake of the gospel, that I may share in its blessings" (1 Cor. 9:19, 22–23).

Allies and collaborators can play strategic roles in the issues we care about deeply. It is to our advantage to seek them out at every opportunity.

5. BE PREPARED TO LOSE SOMETIMES;
EVEN THEN YOU CAN WIN

As noted in chapter 4, the Christian apologist is not always able to persuade the independent relativist to do the moral thing. Sometimes the appeal of self-gratification is just too strong. All the logical reasons why the positions of the Bible do, in fact, make good sense can come up short if the hearer's bias is entrenched. This is not the end of the world. It only means that we go on being the faithful minority. And in so doing, we gain a clearer picture of why we believe as we do and live as we live.

Jesus told his disciples at the Last Supper, "A time is coming when anyone who kills you will think he is offering a service to God. They will do such things because they have not known the Father or me." In other words, don't be surprised when self-driven people act in a self-driven way. He continued: "I have told you these things, so that in me you may have peace. In this world you will have trouble. But take heart! I have overcome the world" (John 16:2–3, 33). One way or another, Jesus manages to come out the winner.

The best illustration of this fact that I have personally witnessed occurred when I was a third-grader in a small Illinois hamlet called Grand Detour, about fifty miles from the Wisconsin line. The year was 1951, and my father was the new pastor of the only active church in this idyllic village, home to maybe three hundred people at best. Five miles south through the cornfields lay the county seat town of Dixon, boyhood home of Ronald Reagan. Nobody talked much about him back in those days; he was just another actor making movies out in Hollywood. They told us instead about the real hero of Grand Detour: the farmer who had come here from Vermont and, in order to break the thick, rich, black Midwestern soil, had in 1837 forged the first steel plow. His name was John Deere. His home and blacksmith shop were still lovingly preserved; you could take a tour there on summer Sunday afternoons.

We had arrived in June. One of the first things my parents did was jump into producing a large and energetic Vacation Bible School. The congregation brought children, both their own and their neighbors', from miles around to listen to Bible stories, make crafts, sing songs, and memorize Scripture verses. This last activity was a big thing with my parents; they had us all write out the verses on three-by-five cards to keep in metal recipe boxes so that we could review them and make sure they stayed firmly in our minds.

"When you go back to school this fall," my mother instructed, "take your verse box with you and put it on your desk as a witness. Then if you have spare time, you can silently go over your verses for reinforcement." She knew how life in a two-room school such as Grand Detour's operated, having taught in similar settings herself. Each teacher had four grades to manage, so that inevitably meant a lot of independent minutes each day for students to complete seatwork assignments and pursue their own projects.

But somewhere along about October a controversy arose. Voices in the little town began to ask why the church kids were bringing those Bible whatevers into the public school. Wasn't that a violation of the law? They must be trying to push their religion onto everyone else....

Down at the Standard Oil station, over at Burgard's grocery, and especially at the little tavern along the river, people talked with furrowed brows. The town fathers were notified that this situation needed looking into. Soon a town meeting was scheduled to sort out whether quiet Grand Detour had on its hands an impermissible breach of the separation of church and state.

Bear in mind, this wasn't liberal Massachusetts or California in the 1990s. This was bucolic Ogle County, Illinois, in the early 1950s!

I didn't get to go to the town meeting; it was for grownups only. My father thought long and prayed hard about what his role should be. Should he even attend? Should he prepare a speech? He knew the opponents viewed him, along with my mother, as the instigators of all this trouble. How should he conduct himself?

In the end, he said he felt that God had led him to go to the meeting—but to say nothing at all. He was the newcomer here; he shouldn't try to railroad his views, especially at the beginning. He would trust that others would speak up, and the outcome would be left to the Lord.

The dramatic evening came. People crowded into the town hall, a squarish white building right next to our church. In fact, we rented it for Sunday school space each week, an arrangement that possibly stood at risk if the evening went badly.

My lanky father slipped quietly through the door at the very last minute and took a seat on a folding chair in the last row. The discussion began with some tension. Several people declared that religion didn't belong in public education; that's what the First Amendment was all about. Others replied that there was nothing official about what the students were doing, and they had a right to bring personal materials to school if they weren't disrupting the educational process. Everyone kept waiting for the new reverend to weigh in on the debate. A few glanced in his direction, then quickly looked away.

They waited in vain. The meeting lasted about an hour and a half altogether, and in the end, people generally came to the conclusion that the goings-on in Mrs. Malach's and Mrs. Callahan's classrooms were not so ominous after all. As long as the kids with the Bible verses in the recipe boxes kept up with their learning and didn't bother anybody else, their freedom should be tolerated.

The meeting adjourned on a relaxed note. People stood up and began to chat about the weather and the crops. My father extended his hand to a few people nearby and said his first words of the entire night: "I'm Ray Merrill. Nice to meet you. What did you say your name was?" After a few minutes of socializing, he donned his hat and disappeared into the night.

I was never as proud of my father as I was when I heard what had happened. He hadn't tried to force anything. He had treated his opponents with respect and even deference. He had modeled the fruit of the Spirit—gentleness, goodness, self-control—that he preached from the pulpit. And in so doing, God's Word had still been allowed its liberty.

But what if the decision had gone the other way? What if the town meeting had concluded that Bible verse boxes were forbidden?

I can tell you exactly what would have happened next. No phone calls would have gone to attorneys. No petitions would have been circulated. No recall efforts would have been launched. Instead, my parents and the lay Sunday school teachers would simply have gathered us kids around them and said, "Now do you see why we memorize the Word of God? We put it deep within our hearts and minds, where no one can take it from us. That's the whole point here. You never know where you'll be in life when you won't have—or people won't let you have—a Bible at hand. So what if they won't let you take your verse box to school? If you have God's truth within you, you're prepared no matter what the circumstances."

We would have felt all the more special, a band of pintsized soldiers bearing the truth whether certain adults liked it or not. We were winners either way.

The words of Titus 3:1–2 are as cogent today, in the midst of our cultural and societal storms, as they were in the first century:

> Remind the people to be subject to rulers and authorities, to be obedient, to be ready to do whatever

is good, to slander no one, to be peaceable and considerate, and to show true humility toward all men.

Such a stance is impervious to the winds of secularism or the fiery darts of Satan. No force can overcome the Christ-followers who draw their strength from the New Testament's timeless words of hope and courage. We Christ-followers in the present decade are not the first to face cultural hostility, and we probably will not be the last. But greater is he who is in us than all the brigades arrayed against us. Christ is our Leader and our Model, and in his name, we must steadfastly persevere to the end.

A Short
"To Do" List
for Christ-Followers

- Pray regularly for the president to hear God's voice.
- Pray regularly for the vice president to hear God's voice.
- Pray the same for your U.S. representative.
- Pray the same for your two U.S. senators.
- Stop telling politician jokes.
- Stop laughing at other people's politician jokes.
- Learn (or learn better) how to share your faith in a natural, positive way. Read a book, ask your church to offer a class, find a mentor in this area.
- At election time, do your homework.
- Vote intelligently.
- If you don't have a clear direction on a given ballot question, leave it blank. Don't just shoot in the dark.
- Make friends with an abortion clinic manager in your area.
- Urge any Christian college with which you have a connection to strengthen its mass media department.
- Nudge your child or grandchild toward thinking about a career in mass media.
- Stop whining about "unfair" news coverage.
- Join the parent-teacher association at your child's school.

- Show up for parent-teacher meetings, conferences, and open houses. Compliment the good you see. If something needs to be questioned, stay respectful and reasonable.

- Women: Ask your obstetrician-gynecologist whether he or she performs abortions. If the answer is no, congratulate the doctor. If the answer is yes, quietly say, "Oh, I'm sorry to hear that." Let the doctor make the next response, if any. (Silence is not bad; your comment will echo in the doctor's mind.) Then tell other Christ-following women what you did. Encourage them to approach their physicians the same way.

- Avoid smart-mouth T-shirts, bumper stickers, and so on.

- Give money to a political campaign you believe in.

- Do some homework, then go to a public meeting (city council, politician's forum) and be a respectful apologist.

- Run for office yourself.

- Encourage a young adult who is depressed about modern life.

- Keep praying.

Notes

ONE: What Is God Thinking?

1. Scott Wesley Brown, Niles Borop, and Dwight Liles, "Look What God Is Doing," copyright © 1988 LCS Songs/Pamela Kay Music/NB Music/Ariose Music.

2. Renee Morris, "There's Going to Be a Revival," copyright 1983 Great Sweetwater Publishers.

3. Leo Tolstoy, *War and Peace,* abr. Edmund Fuller (New York: Scholastic, 1963), 169–73.

TWO: Scorching King Ahab

1. Pat Robertson on *The 700 Club* telecast, 22 January 1995.

2. Congressman Steve Stockman, fund-raising letter for the Coalition of Politically Active Christians (COPAC), October 1996.

3. James C. Dobson, letter to Focus on the Family constituents, July 1996.

4. Eugene H. Peterson, "Teach Us to Care, and Not to Care," Crux 28, no. 4 (December 1992), 124–25.

THREE: Blessings for the Honorable Nero

1. Robert and Cindy Sterling, *The Choice,* copyright © 1992 Word Music, 38.

2. William Law, *The Power of the Spirit* (Fort Washington, Pa.: Christian Literature Crusade, 1971), 72.

3. C. S. Lewis, *God in the Dock* (London: Curtis Brown, 1970), 199.

FOUR: The Christian Stance in a Fallen Society

1. Cited by Steve Chambers, "Polling the Soul," Religion News Service, 15 June 1996.

2. C. S. Lewis, *Out of the Silent Planet* (London: Macmillan, 1973).

3. James Davison Hunter, *Before the Shooting Begins* (New York: The Free Press, 1994), 14.

4. George Barna, *What Americans Believe* (Ventura, Calif.: Regal, 1991).

5. Marvin Olasky, "Victorian Secret," *Policy Review*, Spring 1992, 30.

6. Richard J. Mouw, "Tolerance Without Compromise," *Christianity Today*, 15 July 1996, 34.

7. Philip Yancey, "The Other Great Commission," *Christianity Today*, 7 October 1996, 136.

8. For this outline, I am indebted to my pastor, the Reverend Bob Towell.

9. *Pat Robertson's Perspective* newsletter, April–May 1992.

10. William Law, *The Power of the Spirit* (Fort Washington, Pa.: Christian Literature Crusade, 1971), 123.

11. Charles Colson, "From a Moral Majority to a Persecuted Minority," *Christianity Today*, 14 May 1990, 80.

12. David Rambo, *Leadership*, Spring 1993, 3.

13. Richard J. Mouw, *Uncommon Decency* (Downers Grove, Ill.: InterVarsity Press, 1992), 94.

14. Ex. 9:29; Josh. 3:13; 2 Kings 19:15; 1 Chron. 16:31; 29:11; Job 34:12–13; Pss. 8; 9:7–10; 24:1; 46; 47; 83:18; 89:11; 93:1–2; 96:10; 97:1; 99:1–2; 146:10; Isa. 66:1; Jer. 32:27; Zech. 6:5; Matt. 11:25; Rev. 1:5.

15. Steven Curtis Chapman, "Lord of the Jungle," copyright © 1994 Sparrow Song/Peach Hill Songs (BMI).

16. *U.S. News & World Report*, 15 July 1996, 14.

17. Marcos Witt, "What We Can Learn from the Latin American Revival," *Charisma*, June 1996, 41, 44.

18. Leith Anderson, address at the "Future of the Industry" meeting, Christian Booksellers Association, Colorado Springs, Colorado, 10 March 1995.

FIVE: In Defense of a Little Optimism

1. Aleksandr I. Solzhenitsyn, *The Gulag Archipelago*, pt. 3 (New York: Harper & Row, 1974, 1975), 268.

2. "A Bad Case of the Blues," *U.S. News & World Report*, 4 March 1996, 54.

3. A. A. Milne, *Winnie-the-Pooh* (New York: E. P. Dutton, 1926), 72–74.

4. Eleanor H. Porter, *Pollyanna* (New York: Christian Herald, 1912), 26–27.

5. For the fuller version, see Tony Campolo, *The Kingdom of God Is a Party* (Dallas: Word Books, 1990), 3–9.

SIX: Will We See Thomas Jefferson in Heaven?

1. Cited in Martin E. Marty, *Righteous Empire* (New York: Dial, 1970), preceding contents page.

2. I should not neglect to finish the story: Nearly forty years later my grandfather finally came to the end of his self-destruction, surrendered to Christ, stopped drinking, and became a lay preacher. I remember several warm visits to his humble house, and I had the honor of singing at his funeral, which was officiated by one of his converts.

3. Stephanie Coontz, "Where Are the Good Old Days?" *Modern Maturity,* May–June 1996, 40–41.

4. Marvin Olasky, "Victorian Secret," *Policy Review,* Spring 1992, 30.

5. Coontz, "Where Are the Good Old Days?" 40–41.

6. Published by Basic Books.

7. *Life* 15, no. 25 (20 December 1943).

8. Ibid., 96–97.

9. Ibid., 97.

10. Mark A. Horne, "Were Ozzie and Harriet Good Parents?" *Christianity Today,* 21 June 1993, 40.

11. David Barton, "Questionable Quotes," one-page statement by WallBuilders, 1995.

12. Cited in Bruce L. Shelley, *The Gospel and the American Dream* (Portland, Ore.: Multnomah Press, 1989), 51.

13. Cited in Henry F. May, *The Enlightenment in America* (New York: Oxford, 1976), 280.

14. Cf. Edwin S. Gaustad, "Disciples of Reason," *Christian History* 15, no. 2, 28–31.

15. Marcus Cunliffe, *Washington: Man and Monument* (New York: New American Library, 1958), 60.

16. Mark A. Noll, Nathan O. Hatch, and George M. Marsden, *The Search for Christian America* (Westchester, Ill.: Crossway, 1983), 64.

17. Cited in Edwin Scott Gaustad, *A Religious History of America* (New York: Harper & Row, 1966), 120.

18. Hunter Miller, *Treaties and Other International Acts of the United States* (Washington: Government Printing Office, 1930), 2:365.

19. "A Coppie of the Liberties of the Massachusetts Colonie in New England," in Edmund S. Morgan, ed., *Puritan Political Ideas, 1558–1794* (Indianapolis: Bobbs-Merrill, 1965), 197–98.

20. The Reverend Samuel A. Peters, *General History of Connecticut*, 1781.

21. Samuel Torrey, *An Exhortation unto Reformation*, 8: cited in Thomas Jefferson Wertenbaker, *The Puritan Oligarchy* (New York: Scribners, 1947), 170.

22. William L. Miller, *Piety Along the Potomac* (Boston: Houghton Mifflin, 1964), 41ff.

23. James Davison Hunter, *Before the Shooting Begins* (New York: Free Press, 1994), 230.

24. Os Guinness, *The American Hour* (New York: Free Press, 1993), 184.

SEVEN: Can Any Good Thing Come Out of Washington?

1. *World*, 7 September 1996, 28.

2. "News Hear & There," *Christian American*, July–August 1996, 18.

3. Associated Press citing Gary Bauer, May 1996.

4. Josef Tson, "Thank You for the Beating," *Christian Herald*, April 1988, 28–29.

5. Ibid., 30–32.

6. Peter Ross Range, "The Quitters," *Modern Maturity*, September–October 1996, 40.

7. Ibid.

8. Bruce Barron, "Politics and Religion *Do* Mix," *Christianity Today*, 29 April 1996, 34.

9. *U.S. News & World Report*, 12 June 1995, 94.

10. Cited in Stephen Strang, "Bill Clinton, God's Man?" *Charisma*, March 1993, 10–11.

EIGHT: The Clumsiness of Laws

1. Cited by Will Durant, *The Story of Civilization: Our Oriental Heritage* (New York: Simon & Schuster, 1935), 1:668.

2. Interview by Michael Cromartie, "Equality Is an Illusion," *Books & Culture*, September–October 1996, 19.

3. Interview by Johan Conrod and Tanya Stanciu, "Running the Race," *Rutherford,* August 1996, 15.

4. Paul Weyrich, *Taking Stock* (Washington: Institute for Government and Politics, 1985), 8.

5. Charles Krauthammer, "How Conservatism Can Come Back," *Time,* 18 January 1993, 68.

6. *World,* 12 December 1992, 17.

7. Interview by Michael Cromartie, "How We Muddle Our Morals," *Books & Culture,* May–June 1996, 14–15.

8. Richard J. Mouw, *Uncommon Decency* (Downers Grove, Ill.: InterVarsity Press, 1992), 90–91.

9. James Davison Hunter, *Before the Shooting Begins* (New York: Free Press, 1994), 242–43.

NINE: The Noxious, Necessary News Media

1. "The New America," *U.S. News & World Report,* 10 July 1995, 22.

2. "Our Frightening Episode," *Focus on the Family Citizen,* 24 June 1996, 5.

3. Tim Stafford, "Show Biz Reporters and Jihad Journalism," *Books & Culture,* July–August 1996, 3.

4. Robert Boston, *The Most Dangerous Man in America?* (Amherst, N.Y.: Prometheus, 1996), 15.

5. Joel Belz, "The Messenger, the Message," *World,* 17–24 August 1996, 5.

6. Marvin Olasky, *Telling the Truth: How to Revitalize Christian Journalism* (Westchester, Ill.: Crossway, 1996): cited in Tim Stafford, "Show Biz Reporters," 29.

7. John Milton, *Areopagitica* (1644).

TEN: Where Often Is Heard a Discouraging Word

1. New York: HarperCollins/Regan Books, 1996.

2. Leith Anderson, speech at the "Future of the Industry" meeting, Christian Booksellers Association, Colorado Springs, Colorado, 10 March 1995.

3. Joseph W. Ciarrocchi, "Pastoral Care of Generation X," *Catholic World,* September–October 1995, 218.

4. Taken from *Baby Busters: The Disillusioned Generation* by George Barna. Copyright © 1994, George Barna. Chicago: Moody Press, 1994, 72–74. Used by permission.

5. Ibid., 24.

6. Ibid., 61.

7. Andres Tapia, quoting Danny Harrell, "X-ing the Church," *Christianity Today,* 12 September 1994, 21.

8. Os Guinness, *The American Hour* (New York: Free Press, 1993), 195.

9. Cited in *Leadership*, Summer 1996, 69.

10. "Sex in America," *U.S. News & World Report,* 17 October 1994, 74–81.

11. *New York Times Online,* 7 March 1996.

12. See David Whitman, "The Myth of AWOL Parents," *U.S. News & World Report,* 1 July 1996, 54–56.

13. Associated Press, 18 September 1996.

ELEVEN: Greater Is He

1. Fisher Humphreys, *The Almighty* (Elgin, Ill.: David C. Cook, 1976), 73–74.

2. Richard J. Mouw, *Uncommon Decency* (Downers Grove, Ill.: InterVarsity Press, 1992), 161.

TWELVE: How to Truly Change a Culture

1. Amy Carmichael, *Gold Cord* (Fort Washington, Pa.: Christian Literature Crusade, 1957), 50–51.

2. Amy Carmichael, *If* (London: SPCK, 1938), 8–9.

3. Elizabeth R. Skoglund, *Amma: The Life and Words of Amy Carmichael* (Grand Rapids: Baker, 1994), 18.

4. "Larry King's People," *USA Today,* 28 October 1996.

5. Interview by Johan Conrod and Tanya Stanciu, "Running the Race," *Rutherford,* August 1996, 19.

6. Cited in John Leo, "A New Values Vocabulary," *U.S. News & World Report,* 3 October 1994, 22.

7. Cited in ibid.

8. Garry Wills, "In Praise of Censure," *Time,* 31 July 1989.

9. Gina Kolata, "Under Pressures and Stigma, More Doctors Shun Abortion," *New York Times,* 8 January 1990, A1.

10. As recounted in a speech to the Evangelical Press Association, May 1989, Springfield, Missouri.

11. "Pro-life Counselor's Clever Idea Reaps Abortion Clinic Clients," *Focus on the Family Citizen*, 23 September 1996, 13.

We want to hear from you. Please send your comments about this book to us in care of the address below. Thank you.

ZondervanPublishingHouse
Grand Rapids, Michigan 49530
http://www.zondervan.com